Kettelby, Mary

A Collection of Above Three Hundred Receipts

ISBN: 978-1-948837-13-2

This classic reprint was produced from digital files in the Google Books digital collection, which may be found at http://www.books.google.com. The artwork used on the cover is from Wikimedia Commons and remains in the public domain. Omissions and/or errors in this book are due to either the physical condition of the original book or due to the scanning process by Google or its agents.

This edition of Mary Kettelby's **A Collection of Above Three Hundred Receipts** was originally published in 1714 (London).

Townsends
PO Box 415, Pierceton, IN 46562
www.Townsends.us

A

COLLECTION
OF
RECEIPTS
IN
COOKERY,
PHYSICK *and* SURGERY.

A

COLLECTION

Of above Three Hundred

RECEIPTS

IN

Cookery,

Phyſick *and* Surgery;

For the Uſe of all
Good Wives, Tender Mothers,
and Careful Nurſes.

By ſeveral Hands.

LONDON,
Printed for RICHARD WILKIN, at the
King's Head in *St. Paul's Church-yard.*
MDCCXIV.

THE

PREFACE.

OTHING can be more Self-evident, than that the Usefulness, and consequently the Value of Books of this kind, depend upon the Integrity and Care of the Writers, the Pains they take Themselves, and the good Help and Assistance they can procure from Others. If any of these Requisites be wanting, they must necessarily deceive the Reader; be deceived Themselves; or at best, produce nothing but what's

Mean

PREFACE.

Mean and Trifling, and un-worthy a Publick Reception. There is nothing so easie, as the raising whole Regiments of Nostrums and Recipes, if we will but admit all the Voluntiers of this kind, as fast as they croud in to be listed; but these forward Ones are generally found to fail us in the Time of Trial; and the Success of the Day most commonly to depend upon such, as with great Trouble and Expence are press'd and dragg'd into the Service.

As for my self, I have only to assure the Reader, That as the desire of doing Good, was the sole Motive that at first engaged me in this Work; so has that great Principle ever been too sacred in my Esteem, to suf-
fer.

PREFACE.

fer the least mixture of Unfaith-
fulness or Carelesness through-
out the whole Management and
Composure of it: And farther
to declare, That there has been
no Spare either of Labour, or
Time, or Money, in order to
the making this Collection the
best, and most truly Profitable
in its kind; and that the great
Knowledge and long Experience
of those Excellent Persons who
contributed to its Production,
have abundantly qualified them
for setting the last Hand to such
a Work. To these therefore
are due the greatest Tribute of
Praise, and highest Acknow-
ledgments of Gratitude; who
with a Noble Charity and Universal Benevolence have Expo-
sed to the World such in-

A 4   valuable

PREFACE.

valuable *Secrets,* as *Others*
of a less *generous Temper*
would *have* taken a *Pride,*
and *made* almost a *Merit,* of
Concealing.

And *here* I *freely* own the
greatest share of our *Thanks* to
be *justly owing* to the Fair *Sex;*
who, whether it be from the
greater Tenderness of their
Natures, the *greater* Oppor-
tunities of *Leisure,* or *Advan-*
tages of acquiring *Experience,*
or from *whatever* other *Cause,*
are always *found* most *Active*
and *Industrious* in this, as well
as in all other kinds of *Charity.*
Oh, Heavenly Charity! How
often *have* I *seen* thee *employ*
the *Rich* in *waiting* upon the
Poor, and Mistresses in *Nursing*
and becoming *Hand-maids* to
their

PREFACE.

their own Servants? How often
have I seen thee make Persons
of the Highest Quality Kneel
down to the Dressing of a Poor
Man's Wound: Those of the
greatest Niceness and Delicacy
of Sense, Visit the Chambers of
such, whose Poverty and Offensive Distempers have render'd
them Nauseous and Loathsome
beyond expression: And those of
Tender and Weakly Constitu-
tions walk through Midnight-
Frosts, to the Assistance of some
Poor Neighbouring Woman in
her Painful and Perilous Hour?
And wonderful is the Success
with which Almighty God does
often bless their Labours, (e-
ven in the Use of Plain and
Simple Means) whose Hearts
he first disposes to such Beneficial

PREFACE.

ficial Undertakings. How ear-
neſtly is it to be wiſh'd that
ſuch Examples did more uni-
verſally abound, and that all
our fine Ladies would ſtrive to
adorn their Characters, by
becoming (to uſe the Judi-
cious Mr. Bickerſtaff's Phraſe)
Notable Women?

Nor can I forbear recom-
mending this Generous and Beneficial Practice to the Gentlemen of the Clergy, eſpecially to
thoſe whoſe Pariſhes are remote
from other Help. How ſoon
would their ſuperior Learning
and Sagacity render them Ma-
ſters of this Uſeful Art? How
greatly would the Exerciſe of
it endear them to their People?
What Reverence and Eſteem,
and conſequently, what Oppor-
                              tunities

tunities of doing Good in every other Way, would this procure them? And with what Power and Authority would their Divine Instructions enter into the Hearts of their Audience, when proceeding from the Mouth of such a Benefactor, to whom, under God, perhaps most of them are beholden for their Health, their Limbs, or, it may be, their very Lives? This will be to imitate their Great Master, who went about doing Good, and Healing all those who were Oppressed by the Devil, and who, wherever He met a Patient, seldom fail'd of making a Convert.

I make no doubt, but the Learned Gentlemen of the Faculty will be too Generous to Misconstrue this small Collection of Physical

PREFACE.

Phyſical Receipts, *(deſign'd for the Service of thoſe who are neither within the Reach of their Viſits, nor in a Capacity of Gratifying their Trouble) as an Invaſion of their Province, or a Diſreſpeƈt to their Perſons. I declare my ſelf ſo far from intending either of theſe, that, on the contrary, I eſteem it a great Happineſs and Bleſſing to be able to have a ready and conſtant Recourſe to their Aſſiſtance: And I am proud to own, that moſt of the following* Preſcriptions *came from the moſt Eminent Hands in that Profeſſion. The reſt are all Innocent and Safe; and both the one and the other Approved (not from ſingle Inſtances of Succeſs, but) from a long and repeated Experience.*

The

PREFACE.

The Directions relating to COOKERY are Palatable, Useful, and Intelligible, which is more than can be said of any now Publick in that kind; some great Masters having given us Rules in that Art so strangely odd and fantastical, that 'tis hard to say, Whether the Reading has given more Sport and Diversion, or the Practice more Vexation and Chagrin, in spoiling us many a good Dish, by following their Directions. But so it is, that a Poor Woman must be Laugh'd at, for only Sugaring a Mess of Beans; whilst a Great Name must be had in Admiration, for Contriving Relishes a thousand times more Distastful to the Palate, provided they are but

at

PREFACE.

at the same time more Expensive to the Purse.

I can assure you, that a Number of very Curious and Delicate House-wives Clubb'd to furnish out this Collection, for the Service of Young and Unexperienc'd Dames, who may from hence be Instructed in the Polite Management of their Kitchins, and the Art of Adorning their Tables with a Splendid Frugality. Nor do I despair but the Use of it may descend into a Lower Form, and teach Cook-maids at Country Inns to serve us up a very agreeable Meal, from such Provisions as are Plainest, and always at hand; instead of Spoiling those which are most Rare and Costly, and provoking the Company to pass them

PREFACE.

them away, in *hasty Curses*, to the *Place* from whence the unlucky Proverb *supposes* them to have come; and *so* quit *scores* with him that *sent* them.

The Wines which you are here taught to *Make*, are certainly of the greatest *Perfection* in their *Kind*; their *Flavour* and *Taste* is *Generous*, and their *Ingredients* are *Wholsome*; and *so* lucky have their *Authors* been in their *Imitation*, that many very good *Criticks* have not only *esteem'd* them the genuine *Produce*, but of the nobler *Sorts* too, of the *Foreign Vintages*.

Thus much, I think, may suffice by way of Preface; and *less* I could not possibly *say* with any tolerable *Regard*, either to

the

PREFACE.

the Merits of thofe Worthy
Perfons to whom I am indebted,
or the Intereft of Thofe whom
I am endeavouring to oblige,
who through Ignorance or Pre-
judice, might otherwife have
depriv'd themfelves of fo very
Ufeful and Beneficial an Un-
dertaking.

A
COLLECTION
OF
RECEIPTS.

A Green-Peafe Soop, *without Meat.*

TAKE your Peafe, and in fhelling, feparate the Young from the Old, then boil the Old ones foft enough to ftrain through a Cullender, then put the Liquor and what you ftrained through together : With the Young Peafe whole, add fome whole

B   Pepper,

Pepper, two or three blades of Mace, and fome Cloves. When the laft Peafe are near enough, take fome Spinnage, a little Mint, and a little Green Onion, not fhred too fmall, a little faggot of Thyme and Sweet-marjoram; put thefe into a large Sauce-pan with near a pound of Butter; and as they boil up, fhake in fome Flower to boil with it to the quantity of a Drudging-box full; then put a Loaf of French Bread into the Broth to boil; mingle the Broth and Herbs together: When you have feafon'd it to your Tafte for Salt, add fome fmall White Toafts neatly cut, and the Young Peafe.

A very good Soop.

TAKE a Shin of Beef, a Crag of Mutton or Veal, and a bit of very good Bacon, and half a pound of Rice, fet them on the Fire in as much Water as you think will boil them to Rags; keep it cover'd all the while: When all the Goodnefs of the Meat is out, ftrain it off, and put to it fome whole Pepper,

fome

some Cloves, Mace, and Salt, to your Taste. You may put Soop-Herbs, or a quarter of a pound of plumpt Rice or Verma-jelly; boil a French-Loaf, or two or three Pigeons, for the middle; put in with the Spice a little faggot of Thyme, Savory, and Marjoram: This makes an incomparable Pease-Soop, if you put in a quart of Pease with the Meat at first, instead of Rice.

A *very good* Pease-Soop.

PUT three or four pound of lean coarse Beef, with three pints of Pease, into two gallons of Water; let it boil 'till the Meat is all to rags; and half an hour before you strain it out, put in two or three Anchovies; then strain it from the Husks and Meat, and put into the Sauce-pan as much as you want for that Meal, with an Onion stuck with Cloves, a race of Ginger bruised, a little faggot of Thyme, Savory, and Parsly, and a little Pepper: Let it boil thus near half an hour; stir in a piece of Butter, and fry some

Forc'd-

Forc'd-meat-Balls, Bacon, and French-
Bread cut in Dice, with Spinnage boiled
green, to put to it in the Diſh.

To *make* Craw-fiſh *or* Prawn-Soop.

TAKE ſix Whitings, one large Eel,
with half a Thorn-back, clean
them as to boil, and put them into a
Pot with as much Water as will cover
them ; ſcum them clean, and put in
whole Pepper, Mace, Ginger, Thyme,
Parſly, and an Onion ſtuck with Cloves,
with a little Salt, ſo let them boil to
maſh ; then take fifty Craw-fiſh, or, if
they cannot be got, take an hundred
Prawns, take out the Tails, and pick
out the Bag, and all the woolly parts
that are about the Body ; put all into
a Sauce-pan, with Water and Vinegar,
Lemon, Salt, and a bunch of Sweet-
herbs ; let them ſtew over a gentle Fire
till ready to boil; then take out the
Tails and ſave them carefully, but beat
all the other Shells in the little Liquor
they were ſtewed in, which, with a
French-

French-Roul, you muſt beat 'till the
Shells are extremely fine : When you
have waſhed all the Goodneſs out with
their own Liquor, pour the other Fiſh-
Liquor through the Shells, and ſtrain all
from the Fiſh and Grit ; then have a
large Carp ready ſtewed, and lay it in
the middle of the Diſh ; add the Body of
a Lobſter to the Soop, with ſome ſtrong
Gravy, and burnt Butter ; heat the
Tails of the Craw-fiſh in the Soop, and
pour all over the Carp.

Peaſe-Soop *for* Lent, *or any* Faſting-Day.

PUT a quart of good breaking Peaſe
to three quarts of Water, and boil
them 'till they are tender ; then take
out ſome of the clear Liquor, and ſtrain
the Peaſe as clean as you can from the
Husks. Take ſome Butter and boil it,
and when it breaks in the middle, put
to it an Onion and ſome Mint cut very
ſmall, Spinnage and Sorrel, and a little
Sallery cut large ; ſtir it often, and let
it boil about a quarter of an hour ; then

ſhake

shake in some Flower with one Hand,
and some of your thin Liquor with the
other ; then put in the thick strained
Liquor, some Pepper, Mace, and Salt,
and boil it an hour longer ; then put
into as much as will make a large Dish,
one pint of sweet thick Cream ; put a
French-Roul crispt, and dipt in Milk,
in the middle of the Dish.

To make a Meat-Soop, very good.

TAKE a piece of coarse Neck-Beef,
a Crag of Mutton, and a Knuckle
of Veal ; boil all these to rags, with
Salt, and Onion, and whole Pepper :
When there is no more Goodness left in
the Meat, strain the Liquor into a
Stew-pan, and set it over the Fire ;
put into it Cloves and Mace, and a
little Lemon-peel ; let it boil a little,
then put in a pint of strong Claret,
three or four Anchovies, with Gravy
squeez'd out of a lean piece of Beef
fry'd for that purpose : Put in Ox-Palates
cut in Dice, let them be first boil'd
very tender, Veal-Sweetbreads boil'd,
Lettice,

Lettice, Endiff, Spinnage, or what Herbs you pleafe, boil'd green; then take French-Bread, cut it thin, and toaft it; lay your Palates, Sweetbreads and Herbs over all the Toafts: Have a Fowl boil'd, and the Breaft ftuft with Forc'd-meat, and lay in the middle of the Difh; pour the Soop over all.

To Coller Beef, a very good way.

TAKE a piece of Flank-Beef, cut it fquare, and take off the inner Skin, make a Brine of Water and Bay-falt, ftrong enough to bear an Egg, to the breadth of a Six-pence; let the Beef lie in it one Week, then rub it all over with Salt-petre, and let it lie three Days longer; then take one Ounce of White Pepper, one large Nutmeg, the weight of it in Mace, and the weight of both in Cloves; beat it all grofly and ftrew upon the Beef; then roul it up hard, bind it with a Tape, and few it up in a Cloth, and put it in a long Earthen Pan, fill it up with half Claret and

half

half Water; cover it close with a
coarse Paste, and Bake it twelve Hours
in a very hot Oven; then take off the
Tape and roul the Cloth very hard
about it again, tye it up and hang it
up to drain and cool: If you like
Herbs; Thyme, Sweet-marjoram, and
Parsly shred, are the proper Sort; but
it does not roul so close with as without. It can't be Bak'd too tender.

To make French-Cutlets, *very* Good.

SKIN a Loin of Mutton, and cut
it into Stakes, then take some of
the lean of a Leg of Veal, the weight in
Beef-suet, two Anchovies, Thyme, Parsly,
Sweet-marjoram and Onion, all finely
shred; Nutmeg, Pepper, Salt and grated Bread, with the Yolks of two Eggs;
make holes in the lean of the Stakes
and fill them full of this Seasoning, and
spread it all over the Stakes, then
butter as many pieces of white Paper
as you have Cutlets, and wrap them up
every one by themselves, turn up the
edges

edges of the Papers with great care that none of the Moisture get out; therefore let the Papers be large enough to turn up several times at the edge; and if occasion be, stick a pin to keep it all in; for this Gravy is all their Sauce: When they are thus tight wrapt up, put them upon a Mazareen, and bake them: When they are enough, take them off the Dish they were baked on, and put them on a clean hot Dish; do not take off the Papers but serve them in as they were baked: This is a very delicious Savory Dish, and done with little danger of spoiling, if you wrap them up close. Many People like these best without Sauce; but if you chuse it, let it be strong Gravy, Spice, Onion, shred Capers, Juice of Lemon shook up with a bit of Butter; but they are savory and most whole-some alone.

To

To Coller a Breast of Mutton, to Eat Hot.

TAKE a large Breaſt of Mutton, bone it and take out all the Griſtles, rub it all over with the Yolk of an Egg, ſeaſon it with Pepper, Salt and Nutmeg, Parſly, Thyme, Sweet-marjoram, all ſhred ſmall, Shallot, if you love it, waſh and cut Anchovy in bits, ſtrow all this over the Meat, roul it up hard, tie it with a Tape, and put it into boiling Water; when 'tis tender take it out, cut it in round Slices, not too thin, pour over it a Sauce made of Gravy, Spice, Anchovy, Claret, Onion, a few Sweet Herbs, ſtrain'd and thicken'd with Butter, and ſhred Pickles. Garniſh with Pickles.

To Stew Pigeons.

TAKE ſix Pigeons with their Giblets, cut the Pigeons in Quarters, and put them in the Stew-pan with two blades of Mace, a little Pepper

per and Salt, and juft Water enough to Stew them without burning; when they are tender, thick the Liquor with the Yolk of one Egg, three Spoonfuls of thick fweet Cream, a bit of Butter, and a little fhred Thyme and Parfly; fhake them all up together, and garnifh it with Lemon.

To Broil Pigeons whole.

CUT off the Wings and Neck clofe, leave the Skin at the Neck to tie clofe, then have fome grated Bread, two Pigeons Livers, one Anchovy, a quarter of a pound of Butter, half a Nutmeg grated, a little Pepper and Salt, a very little Thyme and Sweet-marjoram fhred, mix all together; put a piece as big as a Walnut into each Pigeon, few up their Rumps and Necks, ftrew a little Pepper, Salt and Nutmeg on the outfide, broil them on a very flow Charcoal-fire on the Hearth; bafte and turn them very often. Sauce is melted Butter; or rich Gravy, if you like it higher tafted.

To

To Dress a Turbet, *or any Dish of Fish.*

LAY the Fish you are to boil, into a pint of Vinegar, season'd with Salt, Pepper, Onion, and a faggot of Thyme, Marjoram and Parsly; when it has lain an Hour, put the Fish with the Pickle carefully into your Fish-kettle of boiling Water; to it put Cloves, Mace and Anchovies, and a bit of Horse-radish; when they are enough take them out to drain, let the ground of you Sauce be half a pint of the well season'd Liquor in which they were boil'd, and the strain'd Liquor of a quart of Oysters, with half a pint of White-wine, and the Body of a large Lobster; add to it a little more Spice, and a little of Lemon-peal, and one large, or two small Anchovies; then strain it and put to this quantity a full pound and half of Butter; into one piece of which strew as much Flower as will make it of a fit thickness: Your Oysters must be first stew'd, and the Tail and Claws of your Lobster cut in Dice, and both put
into

into the Sauce to heat, when 'tis ready to pour on the Fiſh. Fry'd Smelts, fry'd Parſly, ſcrap'd Horſe-radiſh, and ſlic'd Lemon, with the following Patties is the Garniſh. *Note,* that the Liquor of any well-taſted Fiſh, is more agreeable to the taſte of Fiſh than any Sort of rich Gravy made with Fleſh: And I believe you cannot err, in Dreſſing Fiſh by this Rule for the Sauce. *Note,* Never Boil in too much Liquor, nor too faſt.

Patties, *for a Diſh of Fiſh.*

TAKE Carp or fat Eel, bone and ſhred it very ſmall; to half a pound of this put four ounces of Butter, which you muſt mix in the ſhreding, boil four Eggs in the ſhell, not hard, but as for eating, and put in the Yolks of thoſe Eggs a very ſmall Nutmeg grated, about the weight in Mace, finely beat, as much Salt as both, and a very little Parſly finely ſhred; mix this very well and put them into little ſquare Paſties of hot Cruſt, or Puff-cruſt; if

you

you like it better: Fasten them very
well and fry them in a large Pan-full of
Lard, clarified Butter, Suet or Oil.
You may roul this Forc'd-fish into Balls
with grated Bread; lay them round,
and upon your Fish.

To Pickle Pork, *a good way.*

BONE it, and cut it in such pieces
as will lie most convenient in
your Powdering-tub, which must be
large and found to hold the Meat and
preferve the Brine; the narrower and
deeper your Tub is, the better 'twill
keep the Meat; rub every piece well
with Salt-petre, then take one part
Bay-falt, and two parts common Salt,
and rub every piece very well and cover
it with Salt as you do a flitch of Bacon; then ftrew Salt in the bottom of
your Tub, and lay the Pieces in as
clofe as poffible, ftrewing Salt round
the fides of the Tub: As your Salt
melts on the top, ftrew on more. It
will keep a great while, and is very
good.

To

To Coller a Pig.

SPLIT it up the Belly and Back, then take out all the Bones, wash it clean from the Blood, and lay it to soak in a Pan of Water a Day and Night, shifting the Water as it grows red ; then take it out and wipe it very dry, strew all the inside of both Pieces very well with Salt, Pepper, Cloves, Mace and Nutmeg beat and grated ; then roul them up as hard and tight as you possibly can in two Collars ; bind them with a long Tape as close as 'twill lie, and after that sew them up in Cloths : The Liquor you boil them in must be a quart of White-wine, a little good Vinegar, and the rest Water ; there must be a great deal more than will cover them, because they must boil leisurely above three Hours ; put into the Liquor a piece of Ginger, a Nutmeg cut in pieces, a few Cloves, and two blades of Mace, a sprig of Bays, and a few Leaves of Sage, with some Salt ; when they are tender take them up, and squeeze them tight in the

Cloth,

Cloth, that they may come out in ſhape: When the Liquor they were boil'd in is cold, add half a pint of Vinegar, and keep the Collars in it.

To *make* Veal-Cutlets.

CUT as many Slices of a Leg of Veal as will make a handſome Diſh, beat them with your Rolling-pin, lay them ſingly in a large Diſh, and grate Nutmeg all over them, and ſtrew them with Salt, lard ſome with Bacon, and pour the Yolks of three Eggs well beaten over all; make them all moiſt with the Egg, and fry them of a fine colour in clarify'd Butter; put freſh Frying to every Diſh: When they are all nicely fry'd, put ſome Gravy into the Pan, and the Juice of a Lemon, with Butter and Flower ſhook in; tofs up all 'till 'tis thick, and pour it over the Cutlets; garniſh with bits of Bacon fry'd, and Forc'd-meat-Balls. If it be a Cow-Calf, fill the Udder and Fat with the Forc'd-meat, and roaſt it finely for the middle. Make your Gravy
for

for the Sauce of the Bones and Skins
you do not use; a bit of Beef, Sweet-
herbs, Spice, and White-wine, to make
it look Pale.

To make Dutch-Beef; *a very good Way.*

TAKE eight pound of Buttock-
Beef without Bone, rub it all
over with six ounces of coarse Sugar;
let it lie two Days, then wipe it a
little; then take six ounces of Salt-petre
beaten, a pint of Petre-salt, and a pint
of White Salt, rub it well in, and let it
lie three Weeks, rubbing and turning
it every Day; then sew it up in a Cloth,
and hang it in your Chimney to dry;
turn it upside-down every Day, that
the Brine do not settle. Boil it in Pump-
water 'till 'tis very tender.

C   *To*

To *Fricassey* Chickens, or Sweet-breads.

TAKE two or three Chickens (if small,) wash them clean from the Blood, and cut them to pieces, not too small, set them on in as much Water as will cover them ; when they boil up scum them very clean, then take them out and strain the Liquor; take part of it, to which put some Pepper whole and beaten, a blade or two of Mace, and Salt to your Taste, a little Lemon-peel, a very small Onion stuck with three or four Cloves, a quarter of a pint of White-wine warm'd and put to it ; boil all these together 'till the Chickens are enough ; then take three spoonfuls of Cream, a little Flower mix'd with it and put to the Chickens ; shake it well over the Fire 'till it begins to thicken ; then take the Yolks of two Eggs well beaten, a little grated Nutmeg and Juice of Lemon beat together with the Eggs ; mix these with the Liquor very carefully, by little and little, for fear it curdle ; put in half a pound

of

of good Butter, and ſhake it together
'till that be melted.

Another for the ſame.

TAKE three Chickens, ſtea them,
and cut them into pieces, put
them into a Stew-pan, with as much
Gravy and Water as will juſt cover
them; put in two Anchovies, ſome
whole Pepper, ſome Salt, and a blade
of Mace, a ſmall Onion, with a few
Cloves; ſet them to ſtew, and when
they are almoſt enough, take them from
the Liquor, and fry them in Vinegar,
but a very little; ſtrain the Liquor,
and take as much of it as you ſhall want
for Sauce, and add to it a little Parſly,
Thyme, and Sorrel, boil'd green, and
ſhred ſmall, half a pint of thick Cream,
two Yolks of Eggs well beaten, ſome
grated Nutmeg; ſhake all over the
Fire 'till 'tis thick, throw in half a
pound of Butter, and ſhake it 'till that
is melted,

To Stew a Hare.

PULL your Hare to pieces and bruise the Bones, and put it into a Stew-pan, with three pints of strong Broth, and at the same time put in an Onion, and a faggot of Sweet-herbs; let it stew leisurely for four hours, then put in a pint of Claret; let it stew two or three hours longer, 'till 'tis tender; take out what Bones you can find, with the Herbs and Onions, if not dissolv'd, put in an Anchovy or two with the Claret, Stewing so long, it will be thick enough, you need only shake it up with half a pound of Butter, when ready for the Table.

To Roast a Calf's-Head.

AFTER the Head is nicely wash'd and pick'd, take out the Brains and Tongue; make a large quantity of Forc'd-meat with Veal and Suet well season'd, fill the hole of the Head;

skewer

skewer it and tie it together upon the
Spit: One hour and an half roafts it:
Beat up the Brains with a little Sage
and Parfly finely fhred, a little Salt, and
the Yolks of two or three Eggs: Boil
and blanch the Tongue, cut it in large
Dice, and fry that and the Brains, as
alfo fome of the Forc'd-meat in Balls,
and fome flices of Bacon, The
Sauce is, ftrong Broth, with Oyfters,
Mufhromes, Capers, and a little White-
wine, thicken'd.

To Force a Leg of Lamb.

SLIT the Leg of Lamb down on
the Wrong-fide, and take out all the
Meat, as near as you can, without
cutting or cracking the Out-fide Skin;
beat it very fmall, with its weight in
good frefh Suet; add to it twelve
large Oyfters, two Anchovies, both
neatly wafh'd, and the Anchovies nicely bon'd; feafon it with Pepper, Salt,
Mace, and Nutmeg, a little Thyme
and Parfly nicely fhred; beat all very
fine together, and mix it up with the

C 3 Yolks

Yolks of three Eggs; fill the Skin again with the Meat, and few it up very carefully. The Meat that is left out muft be fry'd for Garnifh to the Loin, which you muft fricaffey as you do Chickens, and lay under the Leg of Lamb. You muft tie the Leg on to the Spit, for any Hole will fpoil the Meat; but 'tis eafie to faften the Back to the Spit with Packthread. In your Fricaffey for this Lamb, leave out the Cream, and add a little Oyfter-Liquor and fry'd Oyfters.

The beft way to Pot Beef, which is as good as Venifon.

TAKE a piece of lean Buttock-Beef, rub it over with Salt-petre; let it lie one Night, then take it out and falt it very well with White and Bay-falt, put it into a Pot juft fit for it, cover it with Water, and let it lie four Days; then wipe it well with a Cloth, and rub it with Pepper finely beaten; put it down clofe into a Pot without any Liquor, cover the Pot
clofe

close with Paste, and let it bake with large Loaves six Hours at least; then take it out, and, when 'tis cold, pick it clean from the Skins and Strings, and beat it in a Stone-Mortar very fine; then season it with Nutmeg, Cloves, and Mace finely beaten, to your Taste, and pour in melted Butter, which you may work up with it like a Paste: Put it close down and even in your Pots, and cover it with clarify'd Butter.

To make Lobster-Loaves.

PICK out all the Meat of three little Lobsters, shred it a little; take a piece of Butter and brown it with Flower in a Sauce-pan; then stir in a very little Onion and Parsly shred very fine, and put in a little Pepper, a spoon-full of Anchovy-Liquor, three or four spoon-fulls of good Gravy, three Yolks of Eggs well beat; stir all these over the Fire in the brown Butter, then put in the Lobster, and stir it a little together: Take three French-Rouls,

C 4 and

and, cut a round Piece off the top of each, and pick out the Crumb, but do not break a hole through the sides of the Bread; fill up the Roul with the Mixture you have prepared; put on the Piece of Top you cut off, close, and tie them round with a piece of Tape: Make some Dripping boiling hot in your Frying-pan: and when you have just dipt the Roul in Milk, throw it into the Pan-full of scalding Liquor: When they are crisp take them out, and take off the Tape: Be sure to put in three times as much Parsly as Onion. Thus you may do *Shrimp* or *Oyster-Loaves.*

To Roast a Breast of Pork.

OUT of your Quarter cut off only a Knuckle, leaving as much Skin on the Breast as you can; take off the Neck, and leave a very large Breast; bone it, and rub it with Salt pretty well all over; then take Sage and a little Thyme shred small, a whole Nutmeg and a little Cloves and Mace finely
beaten;

beaten; ſtrew the Spice and Herbs
very thick all over the Meat, and rub
it in; then roll it tight up, with the
fleſh inward, ſtitch it faſt together, and
roſt it lengthwiſe 'till 'tis full enough
done.

To Haſh a Calf's-Head.

BOIL your Calf's-Head 'till the
Meat is near enough for eating;
take it up, and cut it in thin Slices;
then take half a pint of White-wine,
and three quarters of a pint of good
Gravy, or ſtrong Broth; put to this
Liquor two Anchovies, half a Nutmeg,
and a little Mace, a ſmall Onion ſtuck
with Cloves; boil this up in the Liquor
a quarter of an hour; then ſtrain it,
and let it boil up again; when it does
ſo, throw in the Meat, with a little
Salt to your Taſte, and ſome Lemon-
peel ſhred fine; let it ſtew a little, and
if you pleaſe, add Sweet-breads ; Make
Forc'd-meat Balls of Veal; mix the
Brains with the Yolks of Eggs, and fry
them, to lay for Garniſh. When the
Head

Head is ready to be sent in, shake in a bit of Butter.

To Dress Hogs-Feet *and* Ears, *the best Way.*

WHEN they are nicely clean'd, put them into a Pot, with a Bay-leaf, and a large Onion, and as much Water as will cover them; season it with Salt and a little Pepper; bake them with Houshold-Bread; keep them in this Pickle 'till you want them, then take them out and cut them in handsome pieces; fry them, and take for Sauce three spoon-fulls of the Pickle; shake in some Flower, a piece of Butter, and a spoon-full of Mustard: Lay the Ears in the middle, the Feet round, and pour the Sauce over.

To Collar a Breast of Veal, *to Eat Hot.*

BONE your Veal; take some Thyme, Sweet-marjoram, Pepper, Salt, grated Nutmeg, and beaten Mace, shred Suet, and Crumbs of Bread, with a few Oysters; beat all these in a Mortar, to mix it together; strew it thick over the Veal; then roll it up into a Collar; then sew it tight in a Cloth, and boil it three hours. Make your Sauce as for a White Fricassey, thicken'd with Cream, and Yolks of Eggs, boiling the Bones first for good Gravy; fry the Sweet-bread in Bits neatly cut. Save some of the Stuffing, for Forc'd-meat; to which add Juice of Spinnage, for Colour; and Yolks of Eggs, to make it roll tight, to fry or boil, for Garnish in the Sauce, with the Sweet-bread.

To

To make Stove-Veal.

TAKE a Fillet of Veal of a Cow-Calf, cut away an Inch of the middle Bone on each fide, that the Meat may lie flat in the Stew-pan; cut off the Udder, and flice it in long Pieces, and roll it in Seafoning of Pepper, Salt, Nutmeg, and Sweet-herbs finely fhred; make Holes through the Fillet, and ftick in thefe feafon'd Pieces of fat Udder as thick as you can, 'till the whole is ftuff'd in; then lay Butter in the Pan, and put in the Meat; fet it on a gentle Fire, turning and fhaking it as you have occafion; then fcum off the Fat, and put in one Onion ftuck with Cloves, a Lemon pared, and cut in half, and fqueez'd in: Continue to fhake it. If your Fire be as flow as it ought to be, 'twill take Five Hours to make it ready: One Hour before it is fo, put in a large pint of ftrong Broth. When the Meat is juft enough, fet on a pint of Oyfters, and a pint of Mufh-romes, with a little of the Broth, and two fpoon-fulls of Capers. Let the

Meat

Meat be again clean scum'd from the
Fat, before you use the Liquor; thicken
this with Flower, and pour it into the
Dish to the Meat. 'Tis a grateful, sa-
voury Dish.

To make a Potatoe-Pye.

TAKE two pound of *Spanish* Potatoes, boil them 'till tender ; then
peel them, and slice them the long
way ; lay them in the Dish ; and take
the Marrow of four large Bones, pick
it out of the Bones in large Pieces, and
lay it upon the Potatoes ; put in two
ounces of Preserv'd-Barberries, as much
Citron and Orange-peel, six slices of
Lemon dip'd in Sugar, cut off the
Rind ; put in a quarter of a pint of
Sack : Cover it with Puff-paste ;
and when the Crust is baked, it is
enough : Then cut off the Lid, that it
may cool a little ; and make a Caudle
of half a pint of Sack, half a pound of
Butter, the Yolks of four Eggs, and a
quarter of an ounce of beaten Cinamon :
Take care it does not turn. Make
your

your Caudle very fweet, and pour it into the Pye.

To Stew Carp.

SCALE and wafh your Carps clean before you open them; then flit them carefully, and fave the Blood in Vinegar; take out all the infide with caution, for fear of breaking any thing, becaufe they muft not be wafh'd on the infide; put into their Bellies fome whole Pepper, Salt, and a blade of Mace; cover them in the Stew-pan or Difh, with Claret and half as much Water, Spice, Sweet-herbs, and a bit of Horfe-radifh; Stew them gently, and turn them when they are enough; lay them on the Difh to drain; and boil up the Sauce they were ftew'd in, with two Anchovies, bon'd and wafh'd, the Vinegar the blood was fav'd in, and a pound of good Butter; thick it with a little Flower, before you put in your Butter.

Good

Good Sauce for Boil'd Rabbets, instead of Onions.

BOIL the Livers, and shred them very small, as also two Eggs not boil'd too hard, a large spoon-full of grated white Bread; have ready some strong Broth of Beef and Sweet-herbs; to a little of that add two spoon-fulls of White-wine, and one of Vinegar; a little Salt, and some Butter; stir all in, and take care the Butter do not Oil; shred your Eggs very small.

A pretty Sauce for Woodcocks, or any Wild-Fowl.

TAKE a quarter of a pint of Claret, and as much Water, some grated Bread, two or three Heads of Rocumbole, or a Shalot, a little whole Pepper, Mace, and slic'd Nutmeg and Salt; let this stew very well over the fire, then beat it up with Butter, and pour it under the Wild-Fowl, which being under roasted,

roafted, will afford Gravy to mix with
this Sauce.

To Fry Oyfters, *for Garnifh, for Fifh or Hafh.*

WASH them in their own Liquor,
and dry them very well; then
have fome Yolks of Eggs beat up, with
Spice and Salt finely beat, and Flower
to make it thick enough, to hang on the
Oyfters: Fry them quick, in clarified
Beef-fuet.

A fweet Pye, *which may be made of Young Lamb or Chickens.*

TO two Chickens, you may take
eight ounces of Marrow, or Butter, if that cannot be had; but a Loin
of Lamb wants very little more than
its own Fat: Seafon your Lamb or
Chickens with Salt, Sugar, beaten
Cloves and Mace; lay it into the Difh,
and put in five Yolks of hard Eggs, with
fome

fome of the Forc'd-meat-Balls, made as
follows: Shred a pound of lean Veal,
with a pound and half of Beef-fuet,
a very little Parfly, Spinnage and
Thyme, fhred very fmall, mixed up
with grated Bread, the Yolks of two
Eggs, and feafon it with Cloves, Mace,
Salt and Sugar beat all fine, and colour
it with a little Juice of Spinnage ; make
it into large Balls, and put as many
in as will lie well ; fhred a Lemon-
peel fine and ftrew in; put in alfo fome
Sweet-meats, and a Coffee-cup of Water, with the Juice of a large Lemon ;
cover it with Puff-pafte, and when it
comes out of the Oven, cut off the Lid,
to let the fiercenefs of the Heat go out,
before you put in your Caudle, which
muft be half a pint of White-wine,
thicken'd with the Yolks of three Eggs,
and fweetn'd as you find Occafion.

To *Stew* Herrings.

FIRST broil them very brown,
then have ready fome White-wine
made hot with an Anchovy, a blade of

D   Mace,

Mace, and a bit of Onion, with a little whole Pepper, all ftew'd in the Wine; then cut off the Heads of the Fifh, and bruife them in the Wine and Spice, and take them out again before you put in your Herrings; let them ftew over Coals, in a Difh that they may lie at length in; let them ftew on both fides 'till they are enough at the Bone; take them out, and fhake up the Sauce with Butter and Flower. 'Tis a very good Way to Drefs them.

To make Saufages.

TAKE almoft the double weight of Fat to your Lean Pork, and pick both clean from Bones, Skin and Kernels; fhred it feverally very fine; then mix and fhred it together, and to four pound of this Meat, you may put a very large Nutmeg, the weight of the Nutmeg in Cloves and Mace, and almoft the weight of all the Spice in Pepper; beat all fine, and let your heap of Salt, be as big again as the Spice and Pepper; fhred a large handful of frefh Sage,

Sage, and a little Thyme, very fine; grate two spoonfuls of white Bread, and take two Yolks of Eggs, mix all very well together, and fill your Skins: If you love Oysters, half a pint shred to this quantity, gives it a rich Taste; these roll and fry without Skins, and keep better in a Pot; add the Yolks of Eggs when you use them. *Norfolk* Links are only Fat and Lean Pork, more grosly cut; and the Seasoning, Pepper, Salt, and a large quantity of Sage shred small, and put in large Skins.

To make a Hog-meat-Pye.

TAKE two Buttock-pieces, or Rearing-pieces of Pork, 'tis what Lean is cut off the Gammon on the inside of the Flitch, cut some of the Fat off the end of the Chine, and beat Fat and Lean together very small; season it with Pepper, Salt, Mace and Nutmeg; tie the Meat, when beat and season'd, in a wet clean Cloth, lay it into the Shape you would have it in the Cloth, and cut some long slips of the Chine-fat, to mix

and

and lay between every Layer of the beaten Meat; when 'tis thus laid round and in order, tie it up hard, and lay a heavy weight to press it very hard and close for three or four Hours: Make your Pye, and when you have laid in the Meat, lay half a pound of Butter over the Meat: Just as you set it into the Oven, pour in a quarter of a pint of Claret. When you Draw it, if you find it dry, pour in melted Butter.

Scotch-Collops, *a very good way.*

TAKE a Fillet of Veal, cut away the outside Skin, and cut it out in thin Collops, with the grain, hack them with the back of your Knife; lard some of them with Bacon, and season all of them with Salt, Nutmeg and Thyme, Parsly, and a little Savory; shred all the Herbs very small, then fry them in a good quantity of clarified Butter, till they look of a fine Yellow; take care they are not burnt
Black:

Black: When they are fo done, lay them before the Fire to drain; pour the Butter they were fry'd in from the Gravy, and put to the Gravy three Anchovies, a little ftrong Beef-broth, a little Oyfter-liquor, and Oyfters, with a quarter of a pint of Claret; let your Oyfters ftew thus 'till they are enough, then fhake in five or fix ounces of Butter; rub the Pan firft with Shallot, put in the Yolks of three Eggs, and take care to ftir or fhake it conftantly, for fear of curdling; juft before you pour it out, fqueeze in the Juice of a Lemon, and pour it over the Collops: You muft have Forc'd-meat-Balls and Mufhromes, and fome fry'd Oyfters, with fliced Lemon, for Garnifh.

To Stew Oyfters.

TAKE a quart of Oyfters, and clear them well from bits of Shells and Drofs in their own Liquor; then ftrain that Liquor, and put to it a large blade of Mace, a fmall Nutmeg flic'd, and a little Salt; let your Oyfters boil

in

in this Liquor, and fcum them clean; when they are near enough, put to them fome Parfly fhred fine, and a little Shallot, if you love it, alfo fhred fine, the Yolks of four Eggs, and near half a pound of Butter: fhake it conftantly.

To make Lobfter-Pyes.

WHEN your Lobfters are boil'd, take them clean out of the Shells, flice the Tails and Claws thin; feafon them with Pepper, and a little Mace and Nutmeg beat fine; take the Bodies with fome Oyfters fhred, mix it up with a little Onion fine fhred, a little Parfly fine fhred, and a little grated Bread, and feafon it as the reft; then take the Yolks of raw Eggs, to roll it up in Balls; lay all into the Pye, with Butter at bottom and top of the Fifh; when it comes out of the Oven, pour in a Sauce of ftrong Gravy, Oyfter-liquor and White-wine, thickn'd with the Yolk of an Egg: 'Tis to eat Hot.

To

To Boil a Turky, or any Fowl, with Oyster-Sauce.

WASH your Oysters very clean in
their own Liquor, which Liquor
you muft then ftrain out into a clean
Sauce-pan; put in your Oyfters, with
a bundle of Sweet-herbs, an Onion,
fome Mace, whole Pepper, and a bit of
Lemon-peel: Then take fifteen, if large,
of thefe Oyfters, with a little grated
Bread, twice as much Beef-fuet fhred
fmall, the Yolks of four hard Eggs, two
Anchovies, a very little Onion fine
fhred, Salt, Pepper, Nutmeg, Thyme,
and Winter-favoury; fhred all together
very fine, and mix it up with a Yolk
of raw Egg; ftuff the Turky, or Fowls,
under the Skin on the Breaft; while
they boil, fet your Oyfters for the
Sauce to ftew very gently over the
Fire; when they are almoft enough
take them out, and put in a quarter
of a pint of White-wine, and half a
pint of ftrong Gravy, with an Anchovy, Herbs and Spice, firft boil'd in,
and ftrain'd clean out of the Gravy;

D 4 when

when all this is boil'd together, put in
as much Butter as will make it thick
and well tasted, 'twill take near a
pound to a quart of Oysters: If you
find it so thin as to part, mix a little
Flower in a bit of the Butter, then
throw in your Oysters again, the Juice
of a Lemon, and some shred Parsley to look Green: Pour it over the
Fowl; and Garnish with Oysters and
Lemon.

To make Westphalia-Hams; absolutely the best way to do them.

CUT your Leg of Fat large Pork,
as like a right Ham as you can,
(Black Hogs make the best) hang it
up two days, then beat it very well on
the Fleshy-side with a Rolling-pin; rub
in an ounce of Salt-petre (finely beaten) in every place, so let it lie a Day
and Night; then take an ounce more
of beaten Salt-petre, with two large
handfuls of common Salt, and a handful

ful of Bay-falt, a pound of coarfe Sugar; mix all thefe together, and warm
them thorough-hot in a Stew-pan, but
be fure not to melt it; and while 'tis
hot, rub it all over the Ham very
well, with two large handfuls more
of Salt; thus let it lie 'till it melts to
Brine, then turn it every Day twice,
and bafte it with that Brine for three
Weeks together : Dry it as Bacon.

To Pot Neat's-Tongues, *a better way then Drying them.*

PICKLE them Red, as you do to
Dry; and when you think them
Salt enough to Dry, boil them very
tender; take them up and peel them,
and rub them with Pepper, Cloves,
and Mace all over; then turn them
round into a Pot to bake: Lay them
in fingle Pots on their fide; you muft
cut off the Root as well as Skin, and
cover them with Butter: Bake them
with Brown-Bread; when they come
out of the Oven, pour out the Gravy,
and

and let the fame Butter ferve, when clear'd; if there is not enough, add more clarified.

To Pot Salmon, *as at* New-Caſtle.

TAKE a Side of Salmon, ſcale and wipe it very well and clean, but don't waſh it; Salt it very well, and let it lie 'till the Salt be melted, and drain'd from it, then ſeaſon it with beat Mace, and Cloves, and whole Pepper; lay in three or four Bay-leaves, and cover it all over with Butter; when 'tis well bak'd take it out, and let it drain from the Gravy, then put it into your Pot to keep; and when cold, cover it with clarified Butter. Thus you may do Carp, Tench, Trout, or any firm Fiſh.

To Pickle Mackarel, call'd Caveach.

CUT your Mackarel into round Pieces, and divide one into five or six Pieces: To six large Mackarel you may take one ounce of beaten Pepper, three large Nutmegs, a little Mace, and a handful of Salt; mix your Salt and beaten Spice together, and make two or three holes in each Piece, and thrust the Seasoning into those holes with your finger; rub the Pieces all over with the Seasoning; fry them brown in Oil, and let them stand 'till they are cold; then put them into Vinegar, and cover them with Oil. They will keep, well cover'd, a great while, and are delicious.

To Stew a Rump of Beef.

FIRST boil it more than half e-nough; then take it off the Fire, and peel the Skin off the top: Have ready
some

fome Pepper, beaten Mace, grated Nutmeg, Salt, fhred Thyme, Savory, Marjoram, and Parfly ; ftuff it in large
holes through the Fat; lay the reft of
the Seafoning all over the top ; and to
bind it on, fpread over it the Yolk of
one or two Eggs. Be fure to fave the
Gravy that runs out in Stuffing, to
which add a pint of Claret, and fome
Vinegar : Put it in a deep Pan that will
not be too big, but let the Liquor
come up to the top : Bake it two hours ;
and when you put it in a clean Difh,
pour the Gravy and Wine it was baked
in, all over.

To make a good Forc'd-Meat
for any Ufe.

TAKE a pound of Veal, and full its
weight in Beef-fuet, a bit of
Bacon ; fhred all together, beat it in a
Mortar very fine ; then feafon it with
Sweet-herbs, Pepper, Salt, Cloves, Mace,
and Nutmegs : And when you roll it
up to fry, add the Yolks of two or three
Eggs, to bind it. You may add Oyfters,
or

or Marrow, on extraordinary Occasions.

To Pot Lamprey.

SEASON your Fish with Pepper, Salt, and Nutmeg, a large Onion stuck with Cloves, three spoonfuls of Claret; cover it with Butter, and bake it: When 'tis enough, take it out, and strain it from the Liquor: Pour off the clear Butter, and add it to as much more as will cover the Fish, in a Pan fit to keep it, and bring to Table. Remember always to Clarifie all the Butter you pour over Potted Things.

A Westphalia-Ham-Pye.

BOIL your Ham as tender as you usually do to eat when 'tis cold; bone and skin it; season it with Pepper, Cloves and Mace beaten; put it into very good Crust, or in a Dish cover'd over with Pasty-crust. Before you Lid
it,

it, lay in Butter; and when it comes out of the Oven, put in clarify'd Butter. 'Tis good either Hot or Cold.

To *Pickle* Codlins, *like* Mangoe.

MAKE a Brine of Salt and Water ſtrong enough to bear an Egg, into which put half a Hundred of the faireſt and largeſt Codlins you can get; they muſt be full grown, but not full ripe; let them lie in this Brine nine or ten Days, ſhifting the Pickle every other Day; then dry them, and very carefully ſcoop out the Core: Take out the Stalk ſo whole, as that it may fit in again; and you may leave the Eye in, if you don't put your Scoop quite through: Fill it, in the room of the Core, with Ginger ſliced thin, and cut ſhort, a Clove of Garlick, and whole Muſtard-ſeed, as much as it will hold: Put in the Piece, and tie it up tight. Make your Pickle of as much White-wine-Vinegar as will cover them, with ſliced Ginger, Cloves of Garlick, and whole Muſtard-ſeed: Pour this Pickle boiling-

boiling-hot upon them every other Day, for a Fortnight or Three Weeks. Stone-Jars are beſt for all ſorts of Pickles.

And this is as good a Way as any for a midling large *Cucumber* ; only don't cut them to put the Garlick and Muſtard-feed in ; for they keep much longer, and eat much criſper, if you let them be whole. But neither *Cucumbers, Peaches,* nor *Melons* are comparable to *Codlins,* for imitating the right *Mangoe.*

To *Pickle* Wall-nuts.

TAKE a Hundred of the large *French* Wall-nuts, at the beginning of *July,* before they have a hard Shell : Juſt ſcald them, that the firſt Skin may rub off ; then throw them into Water and Salt for nine or ten Days, ſhifting them every other Day, and keep them cloſe cover'd from the Air ; then dry them : And make your Pickle of two quarts of White-wine-Vinegar, Long-Pepper, Black-Pepper, and Ginger, of each one ounce ; Cloves, Mace, and Nutmegs, of each half an ounce ;

beat

beat the Spice, and with it a large
fpoonful of Muftard-feed; ftrew this
between every Layer of Wall-nuts,
and pour your Liquor boiling-hot
upon them three or four times, or
oftner, if you fee Occafion: Be fure
to keep them clofe ftopt. A fpoonful
of this Pickle is good in Fifh, or any
favoury Sauce. Three or four Cloves
of Garlick do well, if you do not diflike
the Tafte.

To *Pickle* Mufhromes.

GATHER the fmalleft Buttons,
cut off the bottom of the Stalk,
and throw them into Water and Salt;
then rub them with a coarfe Cloth or
Flannel very clean, and throw them
into another Pan of clean Water: Boil
them in Milk and Water: Take them
out upon a clean Cloth: When they are
dry, put them into Glaffes, with White-
Pepper-corns, and a good quantity of
Mace: Pour good Oil on the top of the
Pickle; it keeps them beft; and put
them in as fmall Glaffes as you can, becaufe

caufe they foon decay when they have taken Air.

To *Pickle* Neats-Tongues, *very good.*

L A Y your Tongues twelve Days in common Salt, and Salt-petre, then boil them very tender, and blanch them; cut off the Root, and lay them into a Pot, and pour over them a Pickle made of good White-wine-Vinegar, which you muft boil up with Pepper, Cloves, Mace, and a little Ginger: When 'tis ready to take off the Fire, throw in a piece of Lemon-peel, and three or four Bay-leaves; put it not to the Tongues 'till cool: Tie them clofe from the Air. A little of the Pickle, with good Oil, is their Sauce.

To *Pickle* Pigeons.

B O N E them neatly, and feafon them with Salt, Pepper, Cloves, and Mace; few them up at the Back,

E and

and tie the Neck and Rump; boil them in two quarts of Water, a pint of White-wine, and as much White-wine-Vinegar; put into it a small faggot of Sweet-herbs, and a bit of Lemon-peel. When the Pigeons are enough, take them off the Fire: When they are out, boil and scum the Pickle very clean; pour it not to the Pigeons, 'till 'tis cold.

To *Pickle* Smelts.

GUT and Wash them clean, then lay them in Rows, and put Pepper, Nutmeg, Cloves, Mace and Salt between every Layer of Fish, and four or five Bay-leaves, powder'd Cochineal and Petre-salt beat and mix'd with the Spice: Boil (as much as will cover them) good Red-wine-Vinegar, and put to them when cold. They exceed *Anchovies.*

To

To *Pickle* Oyſters.

TAKE a Peck of very large Oyſters; when carefully open'd without cutting, waſh them three or four times in their own Liquor; ſtrain the Liquor, and put that into a Skillet: When it boils, put in your Oyſters, with half an ounce of White-Pepper, and five or ſix blades of Mace: Let them boil 'till they begin to ſhrivel up; then take them out of the Liquor, and cover them cloſe, while the Spice and Liquor boils a quarter of an hour longer; then pour it on the Oyſters; and always keep them as much from the Air as you can, to keep their Colour.

An Apple-Pudding *to Bake,* *very good.*

TAKE twelve fair large Pippins, coddle them over the Fire very ſlowly, that they do not crack; when they are ſoft, peel and core them, and

E 2　　　　　pulp

pulp them through a Cullender : Add
to this three spoonfuls of Orange-flower-
Water, ten Eggs well beat and strained, half a pound of very good Butter
melted ; make it very sweet, the Apples require it : Add Candy'd Orange,
Lemon, or Citron-peel : Put a Sheet of
Puff-paste into a Dish, and pour in your
Pudding ; bake it with care : 'Tis done
in half an Hour.

The *best* Orange-Pudding *that ever was tasted.*

PARE the Yellow Rind of two fair
Sevil-Oranges, so very thin that
no part of the White comes with it ;
shred and beat it extremely small in
a large Stone-mortar ; add to it, when
very fine, half a pound of Butter, half a
pound of Sugar, and the Yolks of six-
teen Eggs ; beat all together in the
Mortar 'till 'tis all of a Colour ; then
pour it into your Dish in which you
have laid a Sheet of Puff-paste. I
think Grating the Peel saves Trouble,
and does it finer and thinner than you
can

can ſhred or beat it: But you muſt beat up the Butter and Sugar with it, and the Eggs with all, to mix them well.

A Rice-Pudding.

GRIND or Beat half a pound of Rice to Flower, mix it, by degrees, with three pints of Milk, and thicken it over the Fire with care, for fear of burning, 'till 'tis like a Haſty-Pudding: When 'tis ſo thick, pour it out, and let it ſtand to cool: Put to it nine Eggs, (but half the Whites,) three or four ſpoonfuls of Orange-flower-Water: Melt almoſt a pound of good Butter, and ſweeten it to your Taſte. Add Sweet-meats, if you pleaſe.

White Hog's-Puddings.

TAKE a quart of Cream, and four-teen Eggs, (only half the Whites,) beat them but a little; and when the Cream boils, put in the Eggs; keep

them

them stirring on a gentle Fire 'till 'tis all a thick Curd: After 'tis almost cold, put to it a pound of grated White-bread, two pounds of suet shred very fine, two Nutmegs grated, some Citron cut small, half a pound of Almonds beat small, with Orange-flower-Water, Salt, and Sugar to yuor Taste: To this you may put three quarters of a pint of Cream when you go filling.

A Neat's-foot-Pudding.

TAKE to a pound of Neats-foot finely shred, three quarters of a pound of Suet shred as small, a whole Nutmeg grated, Candy'd Orange minced, some Salt, and some Currants, a little grated Bread, and seven Eggs, (leave out half the Whites;) flower the Bag, and let it boil two Hours and a half at least. The Sauce is, Sack, Sugar and Butter melted.

Custards,

Cuſtards, *very good.*

BOIL a quart of Cream, then ſweeten it with fine-powder'd Sugar, beat eight Yolks of Eggs, with two ſpoonfuls of Orange-flower-Water; ſtir this in the Cream, and ſtrain all through a Sieve: Fill your Cups or Cruſt, and bake them with Care.

Orange-Cheeſe-cakes, *very good.*

BLANCH half a pound of ſound Sweet-Almonds, beat them very fine, with two ſpoonfuls of Orange-flower-Water, half a pound of Sugar beat and ſifted, three quarters of a pound of melted Butter: Put to the reſt, when almoſt cold, eight Eggs, leaving out half the Whites; beat and ſtrain them: Boil the Peel of a *Sevil* Orange 'till the Bitterneſs is out, beat it fine, and mix it with the reſt; put it into very light Cruſt: 'Tis an incomparable Cheeſe-cake without the Orange.

E 4   *Another*

Another Cheese-cake, *without* Curd, *very good.*

TAKE a quart of Cream, and seven Eggs, Yolks and Whites; beat three of the Eggs, and put as much Rice-flower to them as will make them thick as a Paste; then put in the other four Eggs, being a little beaten, and stir all well together; set on your Cream to boil, and put in your Eggs and Rice, stirring it all the time, 'till 'tis a pretty thick Curd: When 'tis cold, season one part with a spoonful or two of Sack, Nutmeg, Sugar, and Currants, and the other with Orange-flower-water, Ambergreese, and Sugar; put them in very good Crust: A little time bakes them.

A good Cheese-cake, *with Curd.*

TO a pound and half of Cheese-curd, put ten ounces of Butter, beat both in a Mortar, 'till all looks like Butter; then add a quarter of a pound of

of Almonds, beat with Orange-flower-
Water, a pound of Sugar, eight Eggs,
half the Whites, a little beaten Mace,
and a little Cream, beat all together :
A quarter of an Hour bakes them in
Puff-cruft, and in a quick Oven.

Thin Cream Pan-cakes, *call'd* *a* Quire of Paper.

TAKE to a pint of Cream, eight
Eggs, leaving out two Whites,
three fpoonfuls of fine Flower, three
fpoonfuls of Sack, and one fpoonful
of Orange-flower-Water, a little Sugar,
a grated Nutmeg, and a quarter of a
pound of Butter, melted in the Cream ;
mingle all well together, mixing the
Flower with a little Cream at firft, that
it may be fmooth : Butter your Pan for
the firft Pancake, and let them run as
thin as you can poffibly to be whole,
when one fide is colour'd 'tis enough;
take them carefully out of the Pan,
and ftrew fome fine fifted Sugar between each ; lay them as even on each
other

other as you can: This quantity will make Twenty.

An Almond-Pudding.

BEAT half a pound of good sweet Almonds, with Orange-flower-Water, grated Biskets, three or four, as they are for size, half a pound of Butter, and four large spoonfuls of Sack, eight Eggs, leaving out half the Whites, and a quart of Cream, with Sugar to your Taste; put a Puff-paste at the bottom of the Dish; and Garnish the edge with Paste; so pour it in and bake it: Those that love not Orange-flower-Water, may put a grated Nutmeg instead of it, and beat the Almonds with fair Water, for fear of Oiling.

Orange-

Orange-Pudding.

TAKE three fair Oranges, cut them and squeeze off the Juice into a clean Pan, boil the Peels in two or three Waters, 'till the bitterness is off, then pick out the Pulp and Strings, and beat the Peel very fine in your Mortar, with Orange-flower-Water, then mix it up with the strain'd Juice; add to it nine Eggs, leaving out four Whites, half a pound of Butter, and Sugar to your Taste; put a Puff-paste at the bottom of the Dish; and Garnish the edge of the Dish with Paste: Some People only grate in the Peels raw, and leave out the Juice; but I think the above-written way, is the most Grateful and Pleasant.

A Custard Sack-Posset.

TAKE a quart of Cream, boil it, and season it well with Sugar; then take ten Eggs, with two Whites,
beaten

beaten very well, ftrain them to half
a pint of Sack, ftir the Eggs and Sack
with care over the Fire, 'till 'tis very
hot; then pour in the Cream, holding
it very high, and ftir all very well together; cover it clofe and fet it over
a Kettle of Water, 'till 'tis come as
thick and fmooth as a Cuftard : 'Tis by
much the beft Sort of Poffet that is
made.

Cheefe-curd-Pudding.

TAKE the Curd of a gallon of
new Milk, drain'd from the
Whey, beat it very well in a Mortar,
with half a pound of Butter ; then take
fix Eggs, but three of the Whites, beat
them very well, and ftrain them to the
Curd ; two grated Naple-biskets, or a
Half-penny-Loaf, if they cannot be had,
with half a pint of Flower; mix all
thefe together, and fweeten it to your
Palate : Butter your Patty-pans very
well, fill and bake them : Let not the
Oven be too hot ; turn them out, and
pour over them Sack, Sugar, and Butter

ter melted very thick, cut flips of Candy'd Orange-peel, or Citron, to ftick up in them; and flice blanch'd Almonds, for thofe that have not Sweet-meats.

A very good Tanfie.

TAKE a pint of Milk, and a pint of Cream, about a pint of Juice of Spinnage, which muft be well dried, after wafhing, before you ftamp it; ftrain it and pour it in; beat fifteen Eggs with a little Salt, leave out eight Whites, ftrain them into the other things, put in near a pint of grated Bread or Bifket, grate in a whole large Nutmeg, and as much Sugar as will make it very fweet, thicken it over the Fire as thick as a Hafty-Pudding; put it into a butter'd Difh, and a cool Oven: Half an Hour bakes it.

To

To make Hogs-Puddings.

TAKE the Hog's-Tongue, and some of the Lights, with a piece of Liver; when all is boil'd tender, grate the Liver, and chop the Tongue and Lights very small; put this to a gallon of grated Bread, three Pound of Currants, Mace, Cinamon, Nutmeg, Salt, and Sugar, nine Eggs, leave out four whites, three pound of Suet finely shred; wet it with the top of the Liquor you boil'd your Meat in; it must not be too limber: When 'tis ready, fill your Skins.

Liver-Puddings, *very good*

TAKE the Crumb of a Two-penny White-Loaf grated, a pound of Marrow, or fresh Beef-suet, so finely shred, as to go through a Cullender; take a pound of Hog's-Liver boil'd, grate and sift that very fine; boil a quart of Cream, with a blade of Mace,

and

and fweeten it; grate a Nutmeg, and
put it to the reſt; beat up ſix Eggs
with the Whites, a little Salt, and a
ſpoonful of Orange-flower-Water, mix
all together, and fill your Skins: If you
like Currants, you muſt plump them,
before they go in.

A Sagoe-Pudding.

TAKE half a pound of Sagoe, and
waſh it well in three or four hot
Waters, then put to it a quart of New
Milk, and let it boil together, 'till thick
as Haſty-Pudding; ſtir it carefully,
for 'tis apt to burn; put in a ſtick of
Cinamon, when you ſet it on the Fire;
when 'tis boil'd take it out: Before you
pour it out, ſtir in near half a pound of
Butter, beat nine Eggs, with four
ſpoonfuls of Sack, leave out four Whites,
ſtir all together, fweeten it to your
Taſte, and put in a quarter of a pound
of plump'd Currants; lay a Sheet of
Puff-paſte under, and to Garniſh the
brim.

To *Stew* Golden-Pippins, *a very good way.*

PARE them, and nicely ſcoop out the Core, with a very ſmall Scoop, throw them into Water, to preſerve their colour ; to a pound of Pippins thus prepared, take half a pound of Double-refin'd Sugar, and one pint of Water, boil and ſcum the Syrrop, before you put in the Pippins ; when the Pippins are in, let them boil a-pace, to make them clear, and when they are ſo, put in a bit of Lemon-peel, and the Juice of Lemon to your Taſte.

Hart's-horn, *or* Calf's-foot-Jelly, *the beſt way.*

TAKE to half a pound of good Hart's-horn, three quarts of fair Water, let it boil very ſlowly, 'till above one quart be conſumed ; if you cannot get Hart's-horn, one ſet of Calf's-feet, will make more in quantity,

tity, and tafte almoft as well; the look,
with care, will be the fame; ftrain this
Liquor, and let it ftand to cool; the
ftronger you make your Jelly, the
more Ingredients you may ufe ; to
make it Palatable, when it is fettl'd,
as it will be, the next Day, take off
what is clear of the Hart's-horn, and
of the Calf's-foot-Jelly; you muft take
off the Fat from the top, as well as
leave the Drofs at the bottom; to this
two quarts of ftrong Jelly, you may
put a pint of Rhenifh, and a quarter
of a pint of Canary ; beat up the Whites
of fiveEggs to a froth; ftir all together
with Sugar, to make it very fweet;
mix it well, and fet it on the Fire,
and ftir it 'till it Melts and Curdles;
then put in the Juice of five large Lemons, and a bit of the Peel; let this
boil up, then pour it through your
Jelly-bag, and pafs the firft quart or
two, over and over again, 'till 'tis
perfectly Fine.

F   *To*

To make Almond net, *or* White-Jelly.

BLANCH half a pound of Almonds, and beat them very fine, with a little Orange-flower-Water, juft enough to keep them from Oiling; when they are pounded as fmall as 'tis poffible to do them, mix them up with fome of your Jelly, that is not fo much weaken'd with Wine and Lemon, this will colour a pint and half of the Jelly; pafs this through a very fine Hair Sieve, very often, and ftir it 'till it grows thick, that the colour of the Almond may not fettle to the bottom; pour it into pretty fhaped Glaffes, that it may look handfome, when turn'd out upon China-Plates. This Jelly muft be made very good tafted, tho' you may abate a little of the Wine, and Juice of Lemon; becaufe the Almonds fupplies that want; and then being ferv'd out of the Glaffes, it wants ftrength.

Lemon

Lemon-Cream, *the beſt way.*

TAKE three ſmooth fair Lemons, pare them and ſqueeze out the Juice; cut the Peel in ſmall pieces, and put it to the Juice; for two or three Hours, cover it cloſe; and when it taſtes of the Peel, add to it the Whites of four Eggs, and the Yolks of two, beat this well with two ſpoonfuls of Orange-flower-Water, then put all theſe to a pint of fair Water, ſtrain it, and ſweeten it with Double-refin'd Sugar; ſet it over a gentle Fire, and ſtir it carefully, 'till 'tis as thick as Cream; Put it into your Jelly-Glaſſes.

To make Black-Caps, *the beſt way.*

TAKE a dozen and half of very large French-Pippins, or Golden-Runnets, cut them in half, and lay them with the flat ſide down to the Mazareen, which muſt be large; lay

F 2　　　　　　　them

them single, as close by each other as they can lie; squeeze a large Lemon into two spoonfuls of Orange-flower-Water, and pour over them; shred Lemon-peel very fine, and shake between; and grate Double-refin'd Sugar all over them; put them into a quick Oven, and they are done in half an Hour.

Almond-Cream.

TAKE half a pound of good Almonds, blanch and beat them very fine, with Orange-flower-Water; take a quart of Cream boil'd, cool'd and sweetn'd, put the Almonds into it, and when they are mixt, strain it through a Canvas, then stir it over the Fire, 'till it thickens, and pour it into Glasses; if you love it richly Perfum'd, put in a grain of Ambergreese.

To

To *make* Orange-Cream.

TAKE four Oranges, and grate the Peels into a pint of Water, then fqueeze the Juice into the Water; beat the Yolks of four Eggs very well, and put into the Water; fweeten it very well with double-refin'd Sugar; prefs all hard through a ftrong Strainer, fet it on the Fire, and ftir it carefully all one way, 'till 'tis as thick as Cream; then pour it into your Glaffes.

A very Rich Almond-Cream, *to Jelly.*

MAKE a very ftrong Jelly of Hart's-horn; and that it may be fo, put half a pound of good Hart's-horn to a quart and half a pint of Water; let it boil away near half; ftrain it off through a Jelly-bag; then have ready beaten to a very fine Pafte fix ounces of Almonds, which muft be carefully beat with one fpoonful of good Orange-flower-Water, with fix or eight

F 3　　　　　fpoonspoonfuls of very thick sweet Cream: then take neat as much Cream as you have Jelly, and put both into a Skellet, and strain in your Almonds, sweeten it to your Taste with Double-refin'd Sugar; set it over the Fire, and stir it with Care constantly 'till 'tis ready to boil; so take it off, and keep it stirring 'till it is near cold; then pour it into narrow-bottom'd Drinking-glasses, in which let it stand a whole Day: When you would turn it out, put your Glasses into warm Water for a Minute, and 'twill turn out like a Sugar-loaf. This is call'd *Steeple-Cream.*

To *make* Orange-Posset.

SQUEEZE the Juice of two *Sevil-*Oranges, and one Lemon, into a *China-*Bason that holds about a quart; sweeten this Juice like a Syrop with Double-refin'd Sugar, put to it two spoonfuls of Orange-flower-Water, and strain it through a fine Sieve; boil a large pint of thick Cream, with some of the Orange-peel in it cut thin: When 'tis

'tis pretty cool, pour it into the Bason of Juice through a Funnel, which muft be held as high as you can from the Bason: It muft ftand a Day before you ufe it. When it goes to Table, ftick Slips of Candy'd Orange, Lemon, and Citron-peel on the top.

Poftatia-Cream, *very good.*

TAKE an ounce of the Kernels of *Poftatia*-Nut, beat them fmall with two fpoonfuls of Orange-flower-Water, and four Yolks of Eggs; boil a quart of Cream, and mix all together: When the Cream is fo cool it will not curdle the Eggs, thicken it over the Fire with great Care, and put it into your Glaffes.

To make Fry'd Cream.

TAKE a quart of good new Cream, the Yolks of feven Eggs, a bit of Lemon-peel, a grated Nutmeg, two

F 4

fpoonspoonfuls of Sack, as much Orange-flower-Water: Butter your Sauce-pan, and put it over the Fire; stir it all the while one way with a little white Whisk, and as you stir, strew in Flower very lightly, 'till 'tis thick and smooth; then 'tis boil'd enough, and may be pour'd out upon a Cheese-plate or Mazareen; spread it with a Knife exactly even about half an Inch thick, then cut it in Diamond-squares, and fry it in a Pan-full of boiling sweet Suet.

To make a very good Barley-Gruel.

OF three ounces of Pearl-barley make a quart of Barley-water; shift it once or twice, if it is not white; put to it four ounces of Currants clean pick'd and wash'd; when they are plumpt, pour the Gruel out to cool a little, and beat up the Yolks of three Eggs and put into it, with half a pint of White-wine, and half a pint of new thick Cream, the Peel of a Lemon, and as much Sugar as you like; stir it

gently

gently over the Fire 'till 'tis as thick as Cream. 'Tis a pretty wholefome Spoon-meat for Suppers.

To make the Thick Square Cream-Cheefe, *as at* Newport.

YOU muft get a Vat made a quarter and half high, the Bottom nor Top muft not be faftned in, it muft be Four-fquare, with Holes all over ; then take two quarts of good thick Cream, two quarts of Stroakings, and a gallon of New-Milk, fet it with Runnet as for common Cheefe; when 'tis come, take take out the Curd with a *China*-Saucer, and put it into the Vat, ftrew a little clean dry Salt in two or three places as it is laid in ; and as the Curd finks, fill up the Vat, 'till all the Cheefe is in ; prefs it as other Cheefe : Let it ftand in the Vat two or three Days, 'till all the Whey is out, and turn'd often while 'tis in; falt it two Days : When you take it out, you muft let it dry without rubing ; and make it in *May*. If you defire it exactly Four-fquare, let the Vat be

full

full a quarter and half high, and the
Square want an Inch of a quarter.

To make a pretty sort of Flummery.

PUT three large handfuls of Oat-
meal ground small, into two quarts
of Fair-Water, let it steep a Day and
Night; then pour off the clear Water,
and put the same quantity of fresh Water to it; strain it through a fine Hair-
sieve, and boil it 'till 'tis as thick as
Hasty-pudding; stir it all the while,
that it may be extremely smooth;
(and when you first strain it out, before you set it on the Fire, put in one
spoonful of Sugar, and two of good
Orange-flower-Water.) When 'tis boil'd
enough, pour it into shallow Dishes,
for your Use.

To

To *make* Hart's-horn-Flummery.

PUT a pound of Hart's-horn-Shavings to three quarts of Spring-Water, boil it very gently over a foft Fire 'till 'tis confumed to one quart; then ftrain it through a fine Sieve into your Bafon, and let it ftand 'till cold; then juft melt it over the Fire, and put to it half a pint of White-wine, a pint of new thick Cream, and four fpoonfuls of Orange-flower-Water; fcald your Cream, and let it be cold before you mix it with the Wine and Jelly; put in double-refin'd Sugar to your Tafte, and then beat it all one way for an Hour and an half at leaft; for if you are not thus careful in beating, 'twill neither mix nor look to pleafe you. Let the Cups you pour it into be dip'd in clean Water; for if they are dry, it will not turn out well: Keep it in the Cups a Day before you ufe it. When 'tis fent to Table, you muft turn it out, and ftick it all over the top with blanch'd Almonds cut in Slips. Eat it in Cream, or Wine, which you like beft.

Ta

A Whipt Sillibub, *Extraor-dinary.*

TAKE a quart of Cream, and boil it, let it ſtand 'till 'tis cold; then take a pint of White-wine; pare a Lemon thin, and ſteep the Peel in the Wine two Hours before you uſe it; to this add the Juice of a Lemon, and as much Sugar as will make it very ſweet: Put all this together into a Baſon, and whisk it all one way 'till 'tis pretty thick: Fill your Glaſſes, and keep it a Day before you uſe it; 'twill keep good three or four Days. Let your Cream be full Meaſure, and your Wine rather leſs. If you like it Perfum'd, put in a grain or two of Ambergreeſe.

Panada, *for a Sick or Weak Stomach.*

PUT the Crum of a Peny White-Loaf grated into a quart of cold Water, ſet both on the Fire together,
with

with a blade of Mace: When 'tis boiled
fmooth, take it off the Fire, and put
in a bit of Lemon-peel, the Juice of a
Lemon, a Glafs of Sack, and Sugar to
your Tafte. This is very Nourifhing,
and never offends the Stomach. Some
feafon with Butter and Sugar, adding
Currants, which on fome Occafions are
proper; but the firft is the moft grateful and innocent.

To make Sagoe.

PUT an ounce of Sagoe to a pint of
Water that has been boil'd and is
cold, ftir it carefully 'till 'tis thick;
feafon it with three fpoonfuls of Sack or
White-wine, a bit of Lemon-peel, and
the Juice of a Lemon. Sweeten it to
your Tafte.

To make Salop.

PUT half an ounce of Salop to a pint
of Water, ftir it 'till 'tis thick; and
feafon it with Rofe-water, or Orange-
flower-

flower-water, or Sack: If you like it better, a little Juice of Lemon and Sugar. 'Tis good for Weak or Consumptive People.

To *make* Orange-Marmalade, *very good.*

TAKE eighteen fair large *Sevil*-Oranges, pare them very thin, then cut them in halves, and save their Juice in a clean Veffel, and fet it cover'd in a cool Place; put the half-Oranges into Water for one Night, then boil them very tender, fhifting the Water 'till all the Bitternefs is out, then dry them well, and pick out the Seeds and Strings as nicely as you can; pound them fine, and to every pound of Pulp take a pound of double-refin'd Sugar; boil your Pulp and Sugar almoft to a Candy-height : When this is ready, you muft take the Juice of fix Lemons, the Juice of all the Oranges, ftrain it, and take its full weight in double-refin'd Sugar, all which pour in to the Pulp and Sugar; and boil the whole

pretty

pretty faft 'till it will Jelly. Keep your Glaffes cover'd, and 'twill be a lafting wholfome Sweet-meat for any Ufe.

Lemon-Cakes.

TAKE a pound of double-refin'd Sugar, beat and fift it very fine, wet it with Juice of Lemon, boil it almoft to a Candy-height, then drop it on Plates; fet it in a warm place, 'till they will flip off the Plates. They are grateful, and proper to quench Thirft. You may fhred the Peel very fine, and boil up with one half, if you like it; but add frefh Juice with that, or 'twill be too thick to drop neatly.

Orange-Chips.

CUT off the Peels of very fine Oranges, not too thin, boil them in a large quantity of Water, fhifting them often, that they may not be bitter: When they are tender, dry them,

them, and take their weight in double-refin'd Sugar; boil the Chips and Sugar, when wet, to a Candy, 'till the Sugar be almoft confumed: Lay them thin on Plates, to dry.

Jelly *of* Currants.

TAKE your Currants and ftrip them from the Stalks into a Gally-pot, which Pot you muft put into a Kettle of Water over the Fire 'till they be enough; ftrain them through a Flannel Jelly-bag, but don't fqueeze it; add to the Liquor its weight in double-refin'd Sugar, boil both up for a quarter of an Hour very gently, then put it into Glaffes.

Apricock-Chips.

TAKE the weight of the whole Apricocks in double-refin'd Sugar, then flice them the long-way, but don't pare them; boil your Sugar to a thin
Candy,

Candy, then put the Fruit in, and let them stand on the Fire 'till scalding-hot; lay them thin on Plates, and set them in the Sun to dry, when they have lain one Night in the Liquor.

To *Preserve* Apricocks *in* Jelly.

TO a pound of Apricocks, before they are stoned and pared, take a pound and a quarter of double-refined Sugar; stone and pare your Apricocks, and have your Sugar finely beat; as you pare them, lay some Sugar under and over them: When the Sugar is pretty well melted, set them on the Fire and boil them; keep some Sugar out to strew on them in the boiling, to keep their Colour; and as the Scum rises, take it off very clean, and sometimes turn them with the Ladle, as you see occasion: When they are tender, put them into Glasses. Add to your Syrop a quarter of a pint of Pippin-liquor, and the weight of it in Sugar, and let it boil a-while; put it to your Apricocks: Let your Fire be quick;

G   for

for the fooner any White Sweet-meat
is done, 'twill look the better. You
may let the Liquor run through a
Jelly-bag, if you would have it deli-
cately clear.

Prawlins, *or Fry'd* Almonds.

TAKE a pound of the beft *Jordan*-
Almonds, rub them very clean
from the Duft : Take their weight in
Loaf-Sugar, wet it with Orange-flower-
Water, and boil it to a Syrop; then
throw the Almonds into it, and boil
them to a Candy, conftantly ftirring
'till they are dry; then put them into a
Difh, and take away the loofe Bits and
Knobs which will be about them : Put
the Almonds again into the Preferving-
pan, and fet them on a flow Fire, 'till
fome of their Oil comes from them into
the bottom of the Pan.

To

To *Preserve* Orange-Flowers.

PICK the Flowers, and little O-
ranges and Stalks apart, boil the
Flowers in clear Water 'till they are
tender; boil the little Oranges and
Stalks also in several Waters, 'till the
Bitterness be quite gone: To a pound
of Flowers take three pounds of double-
refin'd Sugar, wet the Sugar with
Water, and boil it to a Syrop; then
drain the Flowers from their Water,
and put them into the Syrop, boil them
a little, and put them into Glasses.

Cakes *of* Orange-Flowers.

TO a pound of Flowers take five
pounds of double-refined Sugar;
dip your Sugar in Water, and lay it in
the Preserving-pan to melt; pick the
out-side Leaves off, boil the Flowers in
Water 'till they are tender, and drain
them well: While they boil, you must
set your dissolv'd Sugar on the Fire, and
boil it to a thick Syrop, and be sure

to

to let it stand to be cold, before you put
in your Orange-Flowers; drop them
nicely on Plates, in round Cakes, and
dry them in the hot Sun, or a Stove.

A very good way to make Con-
ferve of Rofes.

MAKE a strong Infufion of Red
Rofes, with Red-rofe-Water,
as much as you think will boil the
Quantity you intend to make; then
take the frefh Buds of Rofes, and clip
off all the white and withered Leaves;
and boil thefe Buds in the infufed
Liquor, as foft as may be, 'till they are
very tender, and as Red as they were
at firft; then take them out, and
weigh them, and put twice the weight
of Double-refin'd Sugar, and boil it
again, with the Sugar, as faft as can
be, 'till it Jellies; when you take it
out, you may add either Amber, Pearl,
Coral, Gold, or Spirit of Vitriol; thefe
laft Additions, are as well made, when
'tis ufed; becaufe 'tis good for many
Diftem-

Diftempers, and they may be fuited to the Occafion.

A Powder *for* Digeftion.

TAKE a very large Nutmeg, the fame weight in Mace, the fame weight in Anifeeds, and the weight of all the Ingredients of Angelica-feeds; bake all thefe in the middle of a fmall brown Wheaten-Loaf; when 'tis enough, take out the Spice and Seeds, and beat them to a very fine Powder, with Powder of Crab's-Eyes, and double-refin'd Sugar, of each a like quantity, enough to make the Powder Palatable; take as much as will lie on a Shilling, after every Meal. I have known it wonderfully relieve a windy, four, weaken'd Stomach; it muft be continued a Month or two.

To

To Candy *any Sort of* Flowers.

TAKE the beft treble-refin'd Sugar you can get, break it in Lumps,
dip them piece by piece in Water;
put them in a Silver Sauce-pan, or
Bafon, melt them over the Fire; when
it juft boils, ftrain it through a Muflin,
and fet it on the Fire again, and let it
boil, 'till it draws in Hairs, which you
may fee by holding up your Spoon;
then put in the Flowers, of any Sort,
and fet them in Cups, or Glaffes, and
when 'tis of a hard Candy, break it
in Lumps, and lay it as high as you
pleafe: Dry it in a Stove, or the Sun,
and 'twill look like Sugar-candy.

Thick Ginger-bread.

A pound and half of Flower, takes
up one pound of Treacle, almoft
as much Sugar, an ounce of beat Ginger, two ounces of Carraway-seeds,
four ounces of Citron, and Lemon-peel

Candy'd

Candy'd, the Yolks of four Eggs; cut
your Sweet-meats, mix all; and bake
it in large Cakes, on Tin-plates.

Wafers.

DRY your Flower, and make it into
a thick Batter with Cream, put in
Mace very fine beat, a little Sugar to
your Taste; Butter your Irons, and let
them be hot, then put in a Tea-spoon-
ful of the Batter; so bake them with
care, and roll them off the Iron, on a
small Stick.

A good Sort of Portugal Cakes.

TAKE a pound of new Butter, and
six Eggs, leaving out two Whites;
then work it together with your Hand,
'till the Eggs are perfectly mixt in the
Butter; to this put one pound of Loaf-
Sugar sifted, a pound of fine Flower
dry'd, half a pound of Currants, a little beaten Mace, mix all together;

Butter

Butter the Pans; fill and bake them in an Oven that won't colour a White Paper.

A Carraway-Cake, *without Yeast.*

TAKE five pound of Flower, and four pound of Single-refin'd Sugar beat, and finely fifted, mix this with a pound and half of Carraway-feeds; to this Quantity, you muft take four pound of Butter, which muft be work'd in eight fpoonfuls of Orange-flower-Water, 'till 'tis perfectly mix'd, and looks like Cream; break twenty Eggs, but half of the Whites, beat them well; and in beating, add fix fpoonfuls of Sack, ftrew in the Flower, Sugar, and Seeds, by little and little, into the Eggs and Butter, with a pound of Candy'd Citron, Lemon and Orange-peel : Let the firft fiercenefs of your Oven be over, before you put the Cake in, for fear of fcorching; for the Oven muft be hot, and you muft keep beating your Cake, 'till it goes

into

into the Hoop, which muſt be juſt **as**
the Oven is ready.

An excellent Plumb-Pudding.

TAKE one pound of Suet, ſhred
very ſmall and ſifted, one pound
of Raiſons ſton'd, four ſpoonfuls of
Flower, and four ſpoonfuls of Sugar,
five Eggs, but three Whites; beat the
Eggs with a little Salt: Tie it up cloſe,
and boil it four Hours at leaſt.

To make Stone Cream.

TAKE a pint and half of thick
Cream, boil in it a blade of Mace,
and a ſtick of Cinamon, and ſix ſpoonfuls of Orange-flower-Water, ſweeten
it to your Taſte, and boil it 'till thick;
then pour it out and keep it ſtirring 'till
'tis almoſt cold; then put in a ſmall
ſpoonful of Runnet, and put into your
Cups or Glaſſes: Make it three or four
Hours before you uſe it; 'tis good.

To

To make Cracknels.

TO a quart of Flower, take a pound of Butter, half a Nutmeg grated, the Yolks of four Eggs beat, with four spoonfuls of Rose-Water; put the Nutmeg and Eggs into the Flower, and wet it into a stiff Paste, with cold Water; then roll in the Butter and make them into shape; put them into a Kettle of boiling Water; when they swim, take them out with a Skimmer, and put them into cold Water; when they are harden'd, lay them out to dry, and bake them on Tin-plates.

A very good Seed Cake.

TAKE a quarter of a peck of fine Flower, and dry it before the Fire, with three quarters of a pound of Sugar, beat a quarter of a pound of Almonds, to keep them from Oiling, pour in two spoonfuls of Orange-flower-Water, as you beat them, and mix
this

this with the Flower and Sugar, put in the full weight of a pound and half of Butter; rub in one half dry, and melt the other in a full pint of Cream; before you begin to mix, put a pint of good Ale-yeaft, to half a pint of Sack, and let it rife before the Fire; let your Butter and Cream juft melt over a gentle Fire, and when 'tis pretty cool, make a hole in the middle of your Flower, and pour in the Cream and Butter, the Sack and Yeaft, with nine Eggs, leaving out four Whites; beat and ftrain your Eggs, and mix all well together, and fet it to the Fire to rife: When 'tis ready to put into the Hoop, mix in a pound and half of fmooth Carraways, with half a pound of Citron, Orange and Lemon-peel Candy'd; cut this in long bits, and ftrew it in the middle of your Cake: You may put more Sweetmeats, and Ice it, if you defire it very rich.

The

The London-Wigs.

TAKE a quarter of a peck of Flower, put to it half a pound of Sugar, and as much Carraways, smooth or rough, as you like; mix these and set them to the Fire to dry, then make a pound and half of Butter hot over a gentle Fire; stir it often, and add to it near a quart of good Milk or Cream; when the Butter is melted in the Cream, pour it into the middle of the Flower, and to it pour a little Sack, and full a pint and half of very good Ale-yeast; let it stand before the Fire to rise, before you lay them on your Tin-plates to bake.

Egg Minc'd-Pyes.

TAKE six Eggs, boil them very hard, and shred them small; shred the double quantity of good Suet very fine; put Currants neatly wash'd and pick'd, one pound or more if your Eggs were large; the Peel of one

one Lemon very fine fhred, half the
Juice, and five or fix fpoonfuls of Sack,
Mace, Nutmeg, Sugar, and a little
Salt; Candy'd Citron, or Orange-peel,
if you would have them rich.

An extraordinary Plumb-Cake.

TAKE feven pound of fine Flower,
and two pound and half of Butter;
put the Butter into the Flower; feven
pound of Currants, and two large Nutmegs, with half an ounce of Mace,
and a quarter of an ounce of Cloves,
all finely beat and grated; one pound
of Sugar, fixteen Eggs, leaving out four
Whites, put in a full pint and half of
Ale-yeaft; warm as much Cream as
you think will wet it, and pour Sack
to your Cream, to make it as thick
as Batter; beat alfo one pound of Almonds, with Sack and Orange-flower-
Water; but don't let them be fine,
but grofly beat; put in a pound of Candy'd Orange, Lemon and Citron-peel,
or more, if you defire it very rich;
mix all and put it into your Hoop,
with

with a Paste under it to save the bottom. This was given by one of the nicest House-wives in *England*; and is as good as ever was made.

Iceing *for the* Cake.

TAKE the Whites of five Eggs, whipt up to a froth, and put a pound of Double-refin'd Sugar sifted, a grain of Ambergreese, and three spoonfuls of Orange-flower-Water; whip it all the while the Cake is in the Oven; when it comes out of the Oven, Ice it; but set it in no more: Leave out the Perfume, if it be offensive.

Lemon *or* Chocolate-Puffs.

TAKE half a pound of Double-refin'd Sugar, finely beat and sifted, grate into it the yellow rind of a very fair large Lemon; then whip up the White of an Egg to a froth, and wet it with this froth, 'till 'tis as stiff

as

as good working Paſte, lay it on Papers and bake it in a very ſlow Oven; lay ſome round and ſome long: If you make Chocolate, grate about an ounce as you did the Peel.

Almond-Puffs.

BEAT two ounces of blanch'd Almonds, with a quarter of a pint of Orange-flower-Water, and ſifted Sugar, till they are fine; whip up the Whites of three Eggs, and mix them with Almonds, Sugar, and Orange-flower-Water; then add as much ſifted Sugar, as will make it into Paſte; lay it in Cakes, and bake it in a cool Oven.

The Right Dutch-Wafer.

TAKE four Eggs, and beat them very well, then take a good ſpoonful of fine Sugar, one Nutmeg grated, a pint of Cream, and a pound

of

of Flower, a pound of Butter melted, two or three spoonfuls of Rose-water, and two good spoonfuls of Yeast; mix all well together, and bake them in your Wafer-tongs on the Fire. For the Sauce, take grated Cinamon, Sack, and melted Butter, sweeten'd to your Taste.

To make Ratafia-Cakes.

TAKE eight ounces of Apricock-Kernels, or if they cannot be had, Bitter-Almonds will do as well, blanch them, and beat them very fine with a little Orange-flower-Water, mix them with the Whites of three Eggs well beaten, and put to them two pounds of single-refin'd Sugar finely beaten and sifted; work all together, and 'twill be like a Paste; then lay it in little round Bits on Tin-plates flower'd, set them in an Oven that is not too hot, and they will puff up and be soon baked.

The

The Nuns-Bisket.

TAKE the Whites of fix Eggs, and beat them to a Froth; take alfo half a pound of Almonds, blanch and beat them with the Froth of the Whites of your Eggs as it rifes; then take the Yolks, with a pound of fine Sugar, beat thefe well together, and mix your Almonds with your Eggs and Sugar; then put in a quarter of a pound of Flower, with the Peel of two Lemons grated, and fome Citron finely fhred; bake them in little Cake-pans in a quick Oven, and when they are colour'd, turn them on Tins, to harden the Bottoms; but before you fet them in the Oven again, ftrew fome double-refin'd Sugar on them finely fifted. Remember to Butter your Pans, and fill them but half.

Pancakes, *very Good.*

TAKE a pint of thick Cream, three fpoonfuls of Sack, and half a pint of Flower, fix Eggs, (but three H   Whites,)

Whites,) one grated Nutmeg, a quarter of a pound of melted Butter, a very little Salt, and some Sugar; fry these thin in a dry Pan.

To make Good Fritters.

MIX half a pint of good Cream very thick with Flower, beat six Eggs, leaving out four Whites, and to the Eggs put six spoonfuls of Sack, and strain them into the Batter; put in a little grated Nutmeg, Ginger, and Cinamon, all very fine, also a little Salt; then put in another half pint of Cream, and beat the Batter near an Hour: pare and slice your Apples thin, dip every Piece in the Batter, and throw them in a Pan-full of boiling Lard.

A Spinnage-Tart, *very Good.*

TAKE six handfuls of Spinnage, wash it clean, and dry it, pick it clean from Stalks, and the hard Rib
that

that goes up the middle of the Leaf,
fhred it extremely fine as 'tis poffible
to be ; put to it a pint of grated Bread
the lighteft you can get, a pint of very
thick Cream, nine Eggs, (but four of
the Whites,) three fpoonfuls of Orange-
flower-Water, a little Salt, and Sugar
to your Tafte ; it ought to be pretty
fweet : If with your Orange-flower-
Water you beat up two ounces of
blanch'd Almonds, 'tis an incomparable addition to the Tafte. Garnifh the
Brim of your Difh with Pafte, and lay
Slips crofs the Top. Thus you may
make *Couflip-Tart* ; but that being not
fo Juicy, will bear beating in a Mortar.
Heat it with Care before it be put it
into the Difh.

An Almond-Tart, *very Good.*

TO half a pound of Almonds blanch'd,
and very finely beat with Orange-
flower-Water, put a pint of thick Cream,
two large Naple-Biskets grated, and
five Yolks of Eggs, near half a pound
of Sugar ; put all into a Difh garnifh'd

with

with Paſte, and lay Slips in Diamonds
croſs the Top; bake it in a cool Oven,
and when it comes out ſtick Slips of
Candy'd Citron in each Diamond.

To *Preſerve* Golden-Pippins, *the beſt Way.*

TAKE to a pound of Apples a pound
of double-refin'd Sugar, and a pint
of clear Spring-Water, ſet it on the
Fire; neatly pare the Pippins, and take
out the Stalks and Eyes, put them into
the Sugar and Water, cover them cloſe,
and let them boil as faſt as you can half
a quarter of an Hour; then take them
off a little to cool; then ſet them on
again to boil as faſt and as long as they
did before; do this three or four times,
till they are very clear: Cover them
very cloſe, 'till you make the following
Jelly for them.

Codlin *or* Pippin-Jelly.

SLICE a pound of Codlins or Pippins
into a pint of clear Spring-Water, let
them boil 'till the Liquor takes all the
Taſte

Tafte of the Fruit; then ftrain it out, and to a pint of this Liquor take a pound of double-refin'd Sugar boil'd to Sugar again; then put in your Codlin-liquor, boil it a little together as faft as you can; then put in your Golden-Pippins, boil them up faft for a little while; juft before the laft boiling, fqueeze in the Juice of a Lemon; boil it up quick once more; take great care they do not lofe Colour: Take the Pippins out, and put them into the Glaffes with the Jelly. This is the moft grateful Way that ever was invented to Preferve them.

To make Raifon Elder-Wine.

TAKE fix gallons of Water, and boil it half an Hour; and when 'tis boil'd, add to every gallon of Water five pounds of *Maliga*-Raifons fhred fmall; pour the Water boiling-hot upon them, and let it ftand nine Days, ftirring it twice a Day: Boil your Berries as you do Currants for Jelly, and ftrain it as fine; then add to every gal-

H 3

lon

lon of Liquor a pint of Elder-berry-
Juice: When you have ftirr'd all well
together, fpread a Toaft on both fides
with Yeaft, let it work a Day and a
Night, then put it into a Veffel, which
be fure to fill as it works over; ftop it
clofe when it has done working, 'till
you are fure 'tis fine, then bottle it.

Another, very Wholfome.

TO every gallon of pick'd Elder-
berries put a full gallon of Water,
boil them together 'till the Berries are
tender, then ftrain it off through a fine
Sieve; let what will run through, but
don't prefs the Berries; to every gallon
of the Liquor put two full pounds of
good *Lisbon*-Sugar: This fort for pre-
fent Drinking. What you defign to
keep fome Years, muft have two pounds
and a half of Sugar; boil the Liquor
and Sugar together, and fcum it clean
in the boiling as long as any will rife;
when cool, work it with Yeaft for
a Night and a Day; put it into the
Veffel, and when it has done working,
ftop it clofe for five or fix Months;
Bottle

Bottle it then, if fine. This ought to be the conftant Drink for all Gouty People: If well boil'd and workt, it never ferments in the Bottle or Stomach.

Quince-Wine.

CLEAN the Quinces with a coarfe Cloth, then grate them on large Graters; then fqueeze them through a Linen-Strainer, to clear it from the grofs thicknefs; then fqueeze it through a Flannel-Strainer, to clear it from all the Thick that remains: To every gallon of this Liquor put two pounds of fingle Loaf-Sugar; let it diffolve, and pour it off feveral times, as it fettles to the bottom; do this a Night and a Day: When 'tis fine, put it into your Veffel, but don't ftop it down for a Week, nor Bottle it in fix Months; then you may, if 'tis perfectly fine; if not, draw it into another Veffel, and ftop it up again.

Be fure to put all *Englifh* Wines into cool Cellars.

Orange-

Orange-Wine.

TO fix gallons of Spring-Water put twelve pounds of fingle-refin'd Sugar, the Whites of four Eggs well beaten, put thefe to the Water cold; then let it boil three-quarters of an Hour, taking off the Scum as faft as it rifes: When 'tis cold, put in fix fpoonfuls of Yeaft, and fix ounces of Syrop of Lemon, beaten together; put in alfo the Juice and Rind of fifty large Oranges thin pared, that no White-part nor any of the Seeds go in with the Juice, which fhould be ftrained: Let all this ftand two Nights and two Days in an open Veffel, or large Pan, then put it into your clofe Veffel, and in three or four Days ftop it down: When it has ftood three Weeks thus, draw it off into another Veffel, and add to it two quarts of Rhenifh or White-wine; then ftop it clofe again, and in a Month or Six Weeks 'twill be fine enough to Bottle, and to drink in a Month after.

Birch-

Birch-Wine, *as made in* Suffex.

TAKE the Sap of Birch frefh drawn, boil it as long as any Scum arifes; to every gallon of Liquor put two pounds of good Sugar; boil it half an Hour, and fcum it very clean; when 'tis almoft cold, fet it with a little Yeaft fpread on a Toaft; let it ftand five or fix Days in an open Veffel, ftirring it often; then take fuch a Cask as the Liquor will be fure to fill; and fire a large Match dip'd in Brimftone, and put it into the Cask, and ftop in the Smoak, 'till the Match is extinguifh'd, always keeping it fhook, then fhake out the Afhes, and as quick as poffible pour in a pint of Sack or Rhenifh, which Tafte you like beft, for the Liquor retains it; rince the Cask well with this, and pour it out: Pour in your Wine, and ftop it clofe for fix Months, then, if 'tis perfeftly fine, you may bottle it.

Black-

Black-Cherry-Wine.

BOIL fix gallons of Spring-Water one Hour, then bruife twenty-four pounds of Black-Cherries, but don't break the Stones; pour the Water boiling-hot on the Cherries, ftir the Cherries well in the Water, and let it ftand twenty-four Hours; then ftrain it off, and to every gallon put near two pounds of good Sugar, mix it well with the Liquor, and let it ftand one Day longer; then pour it off clear into the Veffel, and ftop it clofe: Let it be very fine before you draw it off into Bottles.

Sage-Wine, *very Good.*

TO twenty-eight pounds of *Malaga-*Raifons, pick'd and fhred, have twenty-eight quarts of Spring-Water well boil'd, but let it be cool as Milk from the Cow before you pour it on the Raifons; then put in half a Bufhel
.of

of Red-Sage grofly fhred; ftir all together, and let it ftand fix Days, ftir-
ing it very well every Day, and cover
it as clofe as you can; then ftrain it off,
and pour it into your Veffel; it will
foon be fine, but you may add two
quarts of Sack or White-wine to fine it:
Raifons of the Sun will do as well as
Malaga, if they cannot be had.

Cherry-Wine, *as in* Kent.

WHEN your Red-Cheries are full
ripe, ftrip them from the Strigs,
and ftamp them, as Apples, 'till the
Stones are broke, then put it into a
Tub, and cover it up clofe for three
Days and Nights; then prefs it in a
Syder-prefs, and put your Liquor again
into a Tub, and let it ftand clofe cover'd
two Days more; then take off the
Scum very carefully, for fear of jog-
ing, and pour it off the Lees into another Tub, and let it ftand to clear two
Days more, then fcum and pour it off,
as before. If your Cherries were full
ripe and fweet, put only a pound and
a half

a half of good Sugar to each gallon of Liquor; ftir it well together, and cover it clofe, and ftir it no more 'till the next Day, then pour it carefully off the Lees, as before; let it ftand again, and do the fame the next Day into the Vef-fel you keep it in: You may repeat this oftner, if you fee the Lees are grofs, and like to make it fret. When 'tis fettled, ftop it up 'till feven or eight Months are paft; then, if 'tis perfectly fine, bottle it; if not, draw it off into another Veffel, and ftop it up as much longer: 'Twill keep Seven Years, if Bottl'd fine, and had not beft be drank 'till 'tis a Year old. Our *Englifh* Wines want only Age, to equal, if not exceed all Foreign Liquors.

Rafberry-Wine, *very Good.*

TO every quart of Fruit, you muft pour, boiling-hot, a quart of Wa-ter; cover it very clofe, and let it ftand twenty-four Hours; then ftrain it, and to three quarts of Liquor put two pounds of good Sugar; ftir it together, and

and fpread a Toaft with Yeaft; fet it to work, and pour it off the Lees; put it into your Veffel, and when it has quite done working, ftop it up: If 'tis fine in fix or feven Months, you may Bottle it, and keep it a Year in Bottles.

Note, You muft at firft watch all Wines: And if you find them Fret, continue to Fine them off the Lees every Day, for fome Time, as faft as any Settles.

White Mead, *very Good.*

TO every gallon of Water put a pint of Honey, and half a pound of Loaf-Sugar; ftir in the Whites of Eggs beat to a Froth, and boil it as long as any Scum arifes: When 'tis cold, work it with Yeaft, and to every gallon put the Juice and Peel of a large Lemon: Stop it up when it has done working, and Bottle it in ten Days.

To

To make Apricock-Wine, *Incomparable.*

TO two gallons of Spring-Water take eight pounds of ripe Apricocks, flice them into the Water, and add to both five pounds of Loaf-Sugar; let all boil, and be nicely fcum'd as faft as it rifes, but let it boil fome time before you begin to fcum; take your Scum off into a clean Sieve, and fet it in a Pot, to fave what Liquor comes from it : When the Wine is clear as you can make it from the Drofs of the Sugar, pour it hot upon the Kernels, which muft be crack'd, and put, with the Shells, into the Pan you defign the Liquor to cool in; ftir it together, and cover it 'till cool, then work it with a Toaft and Yeaft; and in two or three Days, when 'tis fettled, fine it off into your Veffel; let it work as long as it will : When it has done working, pour in a Bottle of Rhenifh or fmall White-wine, and ftop it up for fix Months; then, if very fine, Bottle it, and keep it a Twelve-month longer.

Damfon-

Damson-Wine.

TO every gallon of Water put two pounds and a half of Sugar, which you muſt boil and ſcum three-quarters of an Hour; and to every gallon put five pints of Damſons ſtoned; let them boil 'till 'tis of a fine Colour, then ſtrain it through a fine Sieve; work it in an open Veſſel three or four Days, then pour it off the Lees, and let it work in that Veſſel as long as it will; then ſtop it up for ſix or eight Months, when, if fine, you may Bottle it: Keep it a Year or two in Bottles.

Cowſlip *or* Marigold-Wine.

TO every gallon of Water take two pounds and a half of Sugar, boil this an Hour, and Scum it very well, and pour it boiling-hot upon the Yellow Tops of either ſort of Flowers: To every gallon of the Liquor put half a peck of Flowers nicely cut; let this ſteep all Night, and to each gallon ſqueeze in
two

two or three Lemons, with a piece of
Peel cut thin : When thefe have fteep'd
a Night and a Day, work it with a
Toaft and Yeaft : When you put it in
your Veffel, pour it from the Settle-
ment; and when it has work'd as long
as it will, pour into every gallon one
pint of Rhenifh or White-wine. If 'tis
fine in fix Months, you may Bottle it,
but 'tis beft to drink at three or four
Years old. Either Sort is Cordial,
Wholfome, and Pleafant.

To Improve Syder, *and make it perfectly Fine.*

WHEN 'tis firft made, put into a
Hogs-head fix ounces of Brimftone
in the Stone to Colour it; put a gallon
of good *French*-Brandy highly tinctur'd
with Cochineal; beat one pound of
Allum, and three pounds of Sugar-
candy fine, and put it in when you
ftop it up: When 'tis fine, Bottle it,
which will be in fix Months, This
great Secret is fuccefsfully practis'd by
the *Herefordfhire* Artifts.

To

To make Beer, Wine, or any Liquor, Fine.

SET your Veſſel on two Boards the whole length of the Barrel, and lay upon theſe Boards a large quantity of Bay-ſalt, ſo that the Barrel may be fix'd in the Salt; let it ſtand thus one Fortnight, and 'twill be perfectly Fine, tho' full of groſs Lees before. This certainly clears any Liquor better than Iſinglaſs, and is neater, becauſe 'tis only laid to the Out-ſide of the Veſſel. Pray try before you deſpiſe it, and lay a little under any made Wines at firſt; for if they Fret before they Fine, the Wine is never Good.

To make Milk-Punch

TO two quarts of Water put two quarts of good *French*-Brandy, a dozen and a half of Lemons, three-quarters of a pound of double-refin'd Sugar, and three pints of New Milk;

mix

mix all together, and strain it through a Jelly-bag; put it up often, 'till it looks perfectly clear and fine. You must make it a Day or two before you use it; for it will not keep long Bottled.

To make Strong Mead.

TO four gallons of Water put eighteen pounds of Honey; beat the Whites of four Eggs, stir then in with the Honey 'till it be all melted; scum it well as long as it boils, and be sure it boil an Hour and a half: If you like the Taste, you may put a sprig of Rosemary in the boiling: When it is cold, work it with a Toast spread with Yeast; and when you put it into the Vessel, hang therein one Nutmeg, the weight of that in Mace, and the same quantity in Cloves, with four Races of Ginger, in a bit of Muslin; the Spice must be beaten: put in the Peel of two Lemons. When it has done working, stop it up, and let it stand six Months before you Bottle it.

To

To *make* Goofe-berry-Wine.

TO four pound of Goofe-berries full
ripe put a quart of Water, and to
every gallon of Water put four pound of
Sugar; bruife the Goofe-berries well,
and let them ftand in the Water two
Days, ftirring it twice or thrice a Day,
and then ftrain it through a fine Hair-
bag; then put in the Sugar, and ftir it
very well 'till it is melted: When it is
well mix'd, cover it, and let it ftand a-
while; then ftrain it through a Flannel
Bag into the Vessel: When it has done working, stop it close, and let it stand six Weeks,
or two Months, and if fine, Bottle it.

Nothing of brass must be us'd about any
Wine.

To *make* Elder-flower-Wine.

TO twelve gallons of Water put
thirty pounds of fingle Loaf Sugar,
boil it 'till two gallons be wafted, fcum-
ing it well; let it ftand 'till it be as

cool

cool as Wort, then put two or three
fpoonfuls of Yeaft; when it works, put
in two quarts of Bloffoms, pick'd from
the Stalks, ftirring it every Day 'till it
has done working, which will not be
under five or fix Days; then ftrain it,
and put it into the Veffel: After it is
ftopt down let it ftand two Months,
and then, if fine, Bottle it.

To *make* Ratafia.

TO every gallon of Brandy, put a
quart of the beft Orange-flower-
Water, and a quart of good *French*
White-wine; you muft alfo take care
your Brandy be right and good; to
each gallon of Brandy you muft like-
wife put four hundred Apricock-Stones,
and a pound and a quarter of White
Sugar-candy; juft crack the Stones, and
put them in, Shells and all, into a large
Bottle, which may be very clofe ftopt,
and feal'd down; let it ftand in the
Sun for fix Weeks; take it in every
Night, and in wet Weather, and fhake
it when you take it in, or fet it out:
After this is done, you muft let it
stand

ftand to fettle, and rack it off 'till 'tis
perfectly fine.

Cinamon-Water, *very Good.*

IN two gallons of extraordinary Brandy fteep a pound of good Cinamon
bruifed, there let it lie three or four
Days; then put it into your Limbeck,
with two quarts of Cold-ftill'd Plantain-
water; you may draw as much off as
you put in; and with a quart of the
Smalleft boil up two pound and an half
of double-refin'd Sugar : When 'tis
cold, mix all together for your Ufe :
'Tis a noble Cordial.

A Cordial Orange-Water.

TAKE three quarts of good Brandy,
and the Rinds of a dozen and a
half of Oranges, pare them very thin,
that none of the White go in, let them
fteep in the Brandy three Days and
Nights clofe ftopt; then take five pints
I 3   of

of Fair-Water, and a pound and a half of double-refin'd Sugar: Boil this Syrop half an Hour, and ſcum it as any riſes; then ſtrain it through a Jelly-bag, and let it ſtand 'till cold; then mix it with the Brandy, which muſt be firſt pour'd from the Peels, and ſettled: Keep it for Uſe.

Thus you may do *Lemons*, which is a pleaſanter Cordial.

***

To make Citron-Water.

TAKE Citrons and pare off the outward Rinds half a Finger thick, ſlice 'em thin; and take the Citron Kernels, ſlice them in as you think fit; put as much good Sack as will cover them over the top; put all into a Stone-Jug, and ſtop it very cloſe; let it ſtand in a Cellar five Days, then diſtil it in a Glaſs-Still; let it run into a Bottle wherein is fine Sugar-candy in Powder and Ambergreeſe: Draw off in ſeveral Runnings, and mix it as you like,

To

To make Spirit of Clary.

TAKE a gallon of good Sack, a pint of the Juice of Clary, a pound of Clary-flowers, as many Clove-July-flowers, and half as many Arch-angel-flowers, as many Comfry-flowers, and as many Flowers of Lillies of the Valley; let thefe fteep in the Sack all Night, then put it into a Glafs-Still; the fofter it diftils, the ftronger 'twill be: You muft have great care to keep in the Spirits, by pafting the Still every-where; let it drop through a Bag of good Ambergreefe upon as much fifted White Sugar-candy as you think will fweeten it. 'Tis a very high Cordial.

To make Spirit of Carraways.

TO a quart of true Spirit of Sack put two pounds of good fmooth-fugar'd Carraways, bruife them, and put them into a Bottle, with a grain of the beft Ambergreefe; pour the Spirit on them, and feal the Cork very clofe;

clofe; fet it in the Sun for a Month; ftrain it off, and keep it always clofe ftopt for Ufe. One Spoonful does often give Eafe in the Cholick.

A *Cordial* Black-Cherry-Water, *very Good.*

TAKE two quarts of ftrong Claret, and four pounds of Black-Cherries full ripe, ftamp them, and put them to the Wine, with one handful of Angelica, one handful of Balm, and as much Carduus, half as much Mint, and as many Rofemary-flowers as you can hold in both your Hands, three handfuls of Clove-July-flowers, two ounces of Cinamon cut fmall, one ounce of Nutmegs; put all thefe into a deep Pot, let them be well ftirred together, then cover it fo clofe that no Air can get in; let it ftand one Day and a Night; then put it into your Still, which you muft alfo pafte clofe; and draw off as much as runs good; fweeten it with Sugar-candy to your Tafte. 'Tis good in any Melancholy, or for the Vapours.

A very

A very Rich Cherry-Cordial.

TAKE a Stone-Pot that has a broad Bottom, and a narrow Top, and lay a Layer of Black-Cherries, and a Layer of very fine powder'd Sugar; do this 'till your Pot is full: Meafure your Pot, and to every gallon it holds put a quarter of a pint of true Spirit of Wine. You are to pick your Cherries clean from Soil and Stalks, but not wafh them. When you have thus fill'd your Pot, ftop it with a Cork, and tie firft a Bladder, then a Leather over it; and if you fear it is not clofe enough, pitch it down clofe, and bury it deep in the Earth fix Months, or longer; then ftrain it out, and keep it clofe ftopt for your Ufe. 'Twill Revive, when all other Cordials fail.

A
COLLECTION
OF
RECEIPTS
IN
Physick and *Surgery.*

Strong Palsey-Water.

TAKE the Spirits of five gallons of the best Old Sherry-Sack, distill'd in a Limbeck: Take Cowslip-flowers, the Flowers of Burrage and Buglofs, and of the Lillies of the Valley, of each one handful: Take also Rosemary-flowers,

flowers, Sage and Betony-flowers, of
each one handful: Take each Flower
in their Seafon, and so put into some
of the Spirits aforesaid, in an open-
mouth'd Glafs of near a quart, for that
will hold them all, with the Spirits, 'till
you are ready to diftil the Water; but
this, and the reft of the Spirits, muft
be moft carefully ftopt 'till you use it:
Take Lavender-flowers in their Seafon,
ftrip them clean from their Stalks, and
fill a wide-mouth'd gallon Glafs with
them; pour into them the remainder
of your Spirits; then ftop them clofe
with Cork and Bladder, (as before)
and let them ftand fix Weeks to digeft
in the Sun; then put all together, thefe
and the firft fteep'd Flowers, with all
the Spirits in both Glaffes: Add alfo
Balm, Motherwort, Spike-flowers, Bay-
leaves, and Orange-leaves, if to be had,
of each an ounce, cut fmall, and put
to the former Flowers and Spirits:
Diftil all thefe together in a Limbeck;
make three Runnings of it; firft a
quart Glafs, which will be exceeding
ftrong; then a pint Glafs, which will
be almoft as good; laftly, receive from
it a pint Glafs-full, or as much as runs
ftrong;

ſtrong; for when it runs weak, which
you may know by its Taſte and Colour,
which will be Whiter, let it run no
longer: Put your three Runnings all
together: Then take Citron-peel, the
out-ſide Yellow Rind, or Lemon-peels
thin pared, alſo Pine-ſeeds hull'd, of
each ſix drams; of Cinamon one ounce;
of Nutmegs, Mace, Cardamoms, Cu-
cubies, and Yellow Sanders, each
half an ounce; of Lignum Aloes one
dram; make all theſe into a groſs
Powder, putting among them alſo half
a pound of Jujubes new and good, being ſtoned, and cut ſmall: Put all
theſe Ingredients into a White Sarſnet-
bag, to be hung in the Water afore-
ſaid: Take alſo of Prepared Pearls
two drams; of Prepared Smaragd a
ſcruple, Amber, Greate, Musk, and
Saffron, of each one ſcruple; of Red
Roſes well dried and ſweet one ounce:
Theſe may be put in a little Bag by
themſelves, and hung in the Spirit, as
the other: Cloſe it well, that no Air
gets in, for ſix Weeks; then take out
the Water, and preſs the Bags dry;
keep the Water in narrow-mouth'd
Glaſſes cloſe ſtopt.

The

The Use of the Water.

'Tis so strong and powerful, that it cannot be taken alone, but must be dropt on Crumbs of Bread and Sugar by any One, for Prevention: Take it first and last, and at Four in the Afternoon: Fast always before and after it a full Hour at least. 'Tis of exceeding virtue in all Swoonings, Weakness of Heart, and Decay'd Spirits, in all Palfeys, Apoplexies, both to help in, and prevent a Fit; 'twill also keep all Cold Dispositions off the Liver, restores lost Appetite, and fortifies and strengthens the Stomach; 'twill alone cure a Dropsy, if taken at first, and the Patient be kept from Small and Cooling Liquors.

A second Palsey-Water, *made upon the Ingredients of the first.*

WHEN the first Water has run what is Strong, there will be some Small Water at the bottom of the Limbeck; pour it out from the Herbs and Flowers, and drain them; put them
into

into a gallon of the best Sherry, so let
them stand close stopt five Weeks; then
distil them, and let it run as long as it
continues strong; then pour it into the
Glass where the Sarsnet-bags are, and
let them be in this second Liquor close
stopt six Weeks; then you may use it,
as the former, with Bread and Sugar:
For tho' this is not so powerful as the
former, 'tis too strong to take alone.
Both these are good to bathe Outwardly
the Part affected with Weakness by
Palsey, and generally helps any violent
Pains or Aches that any Part is vexed
with; but because Bathing wastes
most, and this sort is less costly, they
commonly use this second sort for that.

A very good Snail-Water, *for a* Consumption.

TAKE half a peck of Shell-Snails,
wipe them and bruise them Shells
and all in a Mortar; put to them a
gallon of New Milk; as also Balm,
Mint, Carduus, unset Hyssop, and
Burrage, of each one handful; Raisons
of

of the Sun ftoned, Figs, and Dates, of
each a quarter of a pound; two large
Nutmegs: Slice all thefe, and put
them to the Milk; and diftil it with
a quick Fire in a cold Still; this will
yield near four Wine-quarts of Water
very good: You muft put two ounces
of White Sugar-candy into each Bottle,
and let the Water drop on it; ftir the
Herbs fometimes while it diftils, and
keep it cover'd on the Head with wet
Cloths. Take five fpoonfuls at a time,
firft and laft, and at Four in the Afternoon.

A Good Water *for the* Spleen; *a Cordial.*

TAKE four ounces of Harts-horn,
one ounce of Cardamoms, one
ounce of Cinamom, one ounce of Saffron, two handfuls of Red Sage, as
much Balm; fteep thefe twenty-four
Hours in two quarts of Sack, or as
much good Brandy, which you pleafe;
diftil it in a cold Still as quick as you
can, and let it drop on four ounces of
Sugar-

Sugar-candy.   Drink of. this when
Low-ſpirited.

A Good Water *for the* Stone.

TAKE four quarts of White-Thorn-
flowers, infuſe them in two quarts
of ſtrong White-wine, with two ounces
of Nutmeg ſliced; let theſe ſtand two
Days, then diſtil it in a cold Still.
Drink it with Sugar, or without, as you
like beſt.

A Drink *for any* Inward Bruiſe *or* Wound.

TAKE one handful of each of the
Herbs following, *viz.* Wormwood, Comfrey, Throatwort, Wood-
Betony, Plantain, Mugwort, Bonewort,
Scabious, Avens, Wild Hony-ſuckle, Egre-
mony, Bramble-buds, Cinquefoil, Spear-
mint, Senacle, White-bottle, Ribwort,
Daiſy-roots, Dandelion, Buglofs, Hau-
thorn-buds: Put to theſe Herbs two

quarts

quarts of White-wine, and a gallon of running Water, and boil it 'till it be half wasted; then strain it, and add to it a quart of Honey; let that boil in the Liquor some time : When 'tis cold, Bottle it very close, and keep it for Use. 'Twill keep many Years, and is necessary for all Families; two or three spoonfuls of it taken Morning and Night. 'Tis really good for Sores, Wounds, and Hurts New or Old, in Men, Women, and Children : Its Virtues of that kind are too long to mention : It has broke and brought away Inward Imposthumes.

An Excellent Balsom.

TAKE a quart of Spirit of Sack, infuse in it four ounces of Sarsaparilla cut short, two ounces of *China* sliced thin, one ounce of *Virginia* Snakeweed cut small; put all these in a twoquart Bottle, and set it in the Sun, shaking it twice or thrice a Day, 'till the Spirit be tinctur'd as Yellow as Gold; then clear off the Spirit into another Bottle,
and

and put to it eight ounces of Gum-Guaice ; set it in the Sun, as before, shaking it very often, 'till all the Gum be dissolv'd, except Dregs, which will be in ten or twelve Days ; then clear it a second time from the Dregs, and put to it one ounce of Natural Balsom of *Peru* ; shake it well together, and set it in the Sun for two Days ; then put in one ounce of Balm of *Gilead* ; shake all well together once more, and set it in the Sun for a Fortnight ; 'tis then fit for Use, and will keep many Years. Its Virtues are too long to insert : 'Tis good to take Inwardly in most Distempers, and proper for all Sores or Wounds, by pouring in some Drops, and binding Lint thereon. The Dose, taken Inwardly, is from half a spoonful to a whole one, in Sugar, or any Liquid Vehicle, for Consumptions, or any Inward Ulcer : Use moderate Exercise with it.

An Oyl *for any* Bruife *or* Wound.

TAKE of the tender Tops of the Bay-Tree, Red-Sage, Lavender, Wormwood, Plantain, Rue, Tormentil, Scabious, Comfrey, Broom, Rape, Ofman-royal, Southernwood, Camomil, Charity, St. John's-wort, Solaman-feal, Amber, Rofemary, Adders-fpear, Golden-Rod, Herb-Robert, Ground-pine, Sanicle, and Bugle, of each one handful; fhred all thefe very fmall, and infufe them in one quart of Oyl-Olive, and three pints of Neat-Oyl; ftop them clofe in a Glafs Veffel, and let them ftand ten or twelve Days in the Heat of the Sun; ftir them every Night when you take them in: After this, boil it over a gentle Fire 'till the Oyl is Green; then ftrain it clear from the Herbs, and add to the Oyl again, half a handful of the Herbs, as before, fhred, with one ounce of Oyl of Turpentine, One ounce of Natural-Balfom, and one ounce of Oyl of Worms: Digeft all in the Sun, as before; boil and ftrain it, and keep it clofe ftopt for Ufe. It muft be made in *May*.

A Salve

A Salve *for the* King's-Evil.

TAKE one pint of the beſt Sallad-Oyl, four ounces of Red-Lead finely powder'd, as much White-Lead, one ounce of Bees-Wax thinly ſliced, of Frankincenſe and the beſt Maſtick each one ounce, of *Burgundy*-Pitch two ounces; let all be beaten; boil the Oyl and Leads ſome little time together over a gentle Fire; keep the Oyl ſtiring while you add the Wax; then boil theſe together for half an Hour, ſtiring it conſtantly: Take it off the Fire, and ſtir it 'till the Heat is abated; then add your Maſtick, and keep it from the Fire 'till it has done working: Boil it gently again, and put in your Frankincenſe, ſtirring it off the Fire, as you did before: Set it on again, and then add the *Burgundy*-Pitch, as before, with Care; then boil all together, 'till it look like Pitch; ſtir it 'till Cold: Leave your Stick in the Middle, and the next Day ſet it on the Fire to melt the Edges; then take it out, and keep it in an Oyl'd-Paper for Uſe. Let the

K 3 Party

Party afflicted spread a Plaister as big
as the Swelling is, and apply : If it gather to a Head, and break, after you
have wash'd the Wound with warm
Vinegar, apply some Lint rolled in an
equal quantity of the Salve warm'd,
and Honey; spread a Plaister of the
Salve, and when the Corruption is
out, that will heal it.   'Tis Incomparable, and safely may be used for
any Swelling.

A Drink *for the* Evil.

TAKE of White Arch-angel two
handfuls, of Outlandish Sweet
Fennel-feed bruised one ounce, of Li-
corish one ounce ; boil these together
in two Wine-quarts of Spring-water;
stop it close 'till half be consumed :
When cold, strain it from the Ingredients; add to the Liquor two ounces
of Damask-Roses : Let the Party drink
of this Liquor Spring and Fall, five,
seven, or nine Days together, as you
best find it agree, three times in the
Day, a quarter of a pint First and Last,
and at Four in the Afternoon.

A Drink

A Drink *for the* King's-Evil, *and* Cancer.

TAKE Guaiacum one ounce, Saſ-
ſafras, Sarſaparilla, Sharp-pointed-
Dock, and Daiſy-Roots, of each half
an ounce; Arch-angel-Flowers, and
Millepedes, of each two large ſpoonfuls;
Ground-Ivy, and Herb-Robert, of each
one handful :. Bruiſe and ſhred all theſe
Ingredients, and put them to ſteep
one Night in three pints of good clear
New Ale; ſtrain it, and drink no other
Drink for ſix Weeks, Spring and Fall.
You may do a larger quantity at a time
for Man or Woman; but you muſt not
infuſe too much at a time, becauſe the
Herbs are apt to change it. At the
ſame time, if the Swellings are painful,
anoint with *Juice of Rue*, prepared as
follows.

An Ointment *for the* Swellings *in the* King's-Evil.

TAKE two ſpoonfuls of Juice of
Rue, as much Sallad-Oyl, beat
them well together; then ſet it over
the

the Fire, and let it boil flowly half
an Hour; add two ounces of Bees-
wax, let it boil a little with this:
Pour it out, and keep it clofe cover'd.
'Tis an Incomparable Ointment to ufe
all the time you take the Diet-Drink.

A Milk-Water *for* Cancer *or* King's-Evil, *for thofe that cannot drink an Infufion.*

TAKE Roots of Dafies, Burdock,
Guaiacum, Saffafras, Sarfaparilla,
China, Tormentil, and Hounds-tongue,
each two ounces; Selandine, Yarrow,
Plantain, Herb-Robert, Agrimony,
Speedwel, Ground-Ivy, and Cinquefoil, of each a large handful; Arch-
angel-flowers one pint; Sweet-fennel,
and Coriander-feeds, of each one ounce:
Shred and bruife all, and put them to
a gallon of Milk: Draw off as much
as runs good, and drink daily a quarter
of a pint every four Hours: Into each
Draught fqueeze the Juice of a fmall
fpoonful of Millepedes.

An

An Ointment *for the* Evil, *or* Rickets.

TAKE Leaves of Oſmond-royal, St. John's-wort, Wormwood, Centaury, White Hore-hound, Germander, Ground-Pine, Golden-Rod, Carduus, Southernwood, Camomil, Tanſy, Penny-royal, Sage, Mint, Rue, Lillies of the Valley, Angelica, Meadow-Saxifrage, of each one ounce; ſhred it ſmall, and add of Oyl one quart; Deer-ſuet, and Claret, of each one pint; Mace one ounce: Boil theſe 'till all the Watery-part is conſumed: Strain it, and anoint the Belly and Joints with it all the Spring and Fall. This has done great Cures on Weakly Children.

For a Strain.

PUT the Arm or Leg into a Pail of Cold Spring-water, and keep it there 'till the Water be warm; then take it out, and repeat it 'till it be well, which it will be without applying any other Remedy.

A Good

A Good Powder *for* Worms.

TAKE an ounce of Worm-feed, and half an ounce of Rhubarb, beat both to a fine Powder, and take a quarter of an ounce of Powder of Prepar'd Coral; mix all three together, and let the Child take as much of this as will lie on a Shilling, for three Mornings together, drinking a glafs of fmall warm Ale after each Dofe.

Another Powder *for the* Worms.

TAKE an ounce of Sena, a quarter of an ounce of whole Worm-feed, a quarter of an ounce of Tanfy-feed, a quarter of an ounce of Annis-feed, a few Leaves of Wood-Betony; dry all thefe, and beat them together very fine; mix it into a Bolus with Syrop of Turnips. A Child of Nine Years old may take a quarter of an ounce of this Mixture; fo lefs, or more, for any other Age. Drink Water-gruel or Poffet-drink in the working. 'Tis good for Men or Women, as well as Children,

For

For Worms.

BRUISE a pound of Worm-feed, and put it into a large Still full of Spear-mint; draw it off as long as it runs Good : Let the Child drink three ſpoonfuls of this Nine Mornings toge-ther.

For the ſame.

ONE drop of Oyl of Brimftone in a little warm Ale, for three Morn-ings together. Do not exceed one Drop for a Child; three is enough for a Man or Woman.

For the ſame.

TO four pounds of the Husks of Wall-nuts put half a pound of Worm-feed, and as much Flower of Brimftone : Draw it off in a Cold Still, and let a Tea-cup be taken every Morn-ing, for a Month. 'Tis an Excellent Medicine for *Worms*, or *Jaundice*, and has done great Cures,

For

For the same.

TAKE one handful of Spear-mint, as much Plantain, as much Goats-Rue, a spoonful of Plantain-seeds: Stamp all together, and squeeze out the Juice, and take two spoonfuls of it in a glass of Sack, three Mornings together.

For the same; well recommended.

HUSK and Dry an ounce of *Sevil*-Orange-seeds, beat them to a fine Powder, and give as much as will lie on a Sixpence, in a spoonful of Syrop of Peach-blossoms: At the same time, bind the Leaves of the Peach-Tree to the Navil of the Child. If you have no Syrop of Peach-blossoms, use Syrop of Black-cherries.

The Red Powder, *for* Fevers, Small-pox, *or* Surfeits.

TAKE of Carduus, Rue, Red-Sage, Lillies of the Valley, Tormentil, Pimpernel, Dragon, Betony, Angelica, Scabious,

Scabious, Speedwel, of each one handful; *Virginia*-Snake-weed one handful;
Wormwood half a handful; Agrimony
and Verum, of each a quarter of a
handful: Shred the Herbs very ſmall,
and Infuſe them in two quarts of
White-wine, in a Jug, which you muſt
ſtop very cloſe, and ſet nine Days in
the Sun: Then ſtrain the Wine from
the Herbs, and infuſe the ſame quantity
of the freſh Herbs in the ſame Wine;
let it ſtand, as before, nine Days more:
Then take a pound of Bole-armoniac
finely powder'd; then put as much of
the Wine (after it is a ſecond time
preſſed out) as the Powder will take
up, and ſet it in the Sun to dry; and
as it dries up, put in more of the
Wine, ſtirring it two or three times
a Day, 'till all the Wine be dried up
in the Powder, ſo as to be fit to
work like Paſte: Then put to it
one ounce of Diaſcordium, and one
ounce of Methridate, half an ounce of
Cochineal, one ounce of Powder of
Red Coral, one ounce of Prepar'd Saffron, forty grains of Bezoar, one ounce
of Powder of Crabs-eyes, one ounce of
Burn'd Harts-horn, and one ounce of
Prepar'd

Prepar'd Pearl; mix these in the last
Wetting, and work them all together:
Make them up in Balls, (when well
mix'd) and dry them in the Sun. Take
forty or fifty grains of this for a Dose.
Drink Mace-Ale after it.

Of Gascoign Powder, *a good Sort for the same Uses.*

TAKE Prepar'd Crabs-eyes, Red
Coral, White Amber very finely
powder'd, of each half an ounce; Burnt
Harts-horn half an ounce, one ounce of
Pearls very finely powder'd, one ounce
of Oriental Bezoar, of the Black Tops
of Crabs-claws finely powder'd four
ounces; grind all these on a Marble-
Stone 'till they cast a Greenish Colour;
then make it into Balls with Jelly
made of *English* Vipers-Skin, which
may be made and will Jelly like Harts-
horn.

A very

A very good Powder *for a* Diz-zinefs in the Head, *and to* Prevent Apoplectick Fits.

TAKE the Seeds and Roots of Single Piony of each a like quantity, dry and beat them feverally into a fine Powder ; take the weight in Nutmeg, which you muft beat, and dry, and beat again ; mix fine-fifted Sugar, and take as much as will lie on a Shilling every Morning for a Month conftantly.

A Powder *to Stop a* Hickock *in Man, Woman, or Child.*

PUT as much Dill-feed finely powder'd as will lie on a Shilling, into two fpoonfuls of Syrop of Black Cherries, and take it prefently.

An

An Excellent Powder *for* Convulsion-Fits.

TAKE two drams of Piony-roots, Miſſletoe of the Oak one dram; Prepar'd Pearl, White Amber Prepar'd, and Coral Prepar'd, of each half a dram; Bezoar two grains, and five leaves of Gold; make all theſe into a very fine Powder, and give as much of it as will lie on a Three-pence to a Child of a Month old, and proportionable to a bigger: Mix it up with a ſpoonful of Black-cherry-Water, which ſweeten with the Syrop of Black-Cherries: Take it three Days together at every Change of the Moon, to prevent Returns.

A Powder *for* Digeſtion.

TAKE Gallingale and Setwal of each one ounce; Long-Pepper, Mace, and Nutmeg, of each two ounces; Annis-ſeeds, Carraway-ſeeds, Fennel-ſeeds, and Angelica-ſeeds, of each

each half an ounce: Put to theſe, all finely powder'd, the weight in fine powder'd Sugar ; take as much as will lie on a Shilling after every Meal, and Drink a glaſs of Simple Carduus-Water after it: This has done mighty Cures to weak deprav'd Stomachs.

A Preſent Remedy for Con-vulſion Fits.

MAKE a Draught of an equal quantity of Piony and Simple Black-Cherry-Water ; and for a Man put thirty, for a Woman twenty, for a Child five drops of Spirit of Hart's-horn ; Drink this in or before a Fit.

Another for the ſame.

INFUSE Turnips in a Pot cloſe ſtopt, and ſet into a Kettle of Wa-ter, 'till they are tender enough to ſqueeze ; then take the Liquor clear from them, and take three ſpoonfuls of it, in one ſpoonful of rich Old *Mala-*
L   *ga ;*

ga: It has Cured the Falling-Sickness in grown-up People; but is almost Infallible for Children.

A Syrop *for* Convulsion Fits.

TAKE one pint of small Black-Cherry-Water, two pounds of Black Cherries, bruise them Stones and all in a Mortar; put these with the Water into a Jug, with two blades of Mace, and four tops of Spear-mint; stop the Jugg close, and set it into a Kettle of Water: Let it simper three Hours over the Fire, then strain it out, and let it be boil'd to a Syrop, with a full pound and half of *Lisbon* Sugar to each pint of that Liquor.

For Convulsions *or* Vertigo.

TAKE one ounce of Juniper-Berries, two ounces of fresh *Sevil* Orange-peel, Male-Piony-roots three ounces, Peacocks Dung six ounces, Sugar-gar-Candy half a pound; Infuse these in two quarts of Rhenish, for twenty-four Hours, in hot Ashes; then let it settle, and take two spoonfuls of this in a glass of Angelica-Water: It has done great Cures.

A *Strong* Milk-Water.

TAKE Mint, Sage and Balm, of each two good handfuls, Rue, Carduus, Wormwood, and Meadow-sweet of each one handful; chop these Herbs together, and put them with four quarts of New Milk, and a whole Nutmeg slic'd, into a Copper Limbeck; from this Quantity you may draw two quarts, if you keep an even slow fire, 'till that Quantity is drawn off: When you have drawn off what you design, mix it all together, for the Use of any Feverish or Consumptive Person.

The

The Barley Cinamon-Water.

PUT two pounds of Pearl Barley, into four quarts of Spring-Water, draw it off in a cold Still, as long as it runs sweet; Infuse in it half a pound of Cinamon, and a quart of Canary; Sweeten it, and Drink a Draught at any time, in a Fever and Looseness.

Wall-nut-Water.

GATHER a large quantity of Green Wall-nuts, in the beginning of *June*, break them in a Mortar, and distil them in a cold Still; keep this Water by itself, and at *Midsummer* do the like, keeping that Water by itself also; about a Fortnight after *Midsummer* do the like; and so again a Fortnight after that; then put all the four Sorts of Water together, and distil it off; keep it close for Use; its Perfections are many: 'Tis good in Consumption and Surfeits; Drank with

Wine

Wine in a Morning, 'tis good for a Pal-
ſey. A Bottle or two in a Veſſel of
decay'd Wine, revives it : It's good to
waſh the Eyes and Temples. I have
not met with any Simple Water ſo
well recommended, or by a Perſon of
more Experience.

A very good Snail-Water.

TAKE a peck of Snails clean wip'd,
crack them and put them into a
gallon of Milk, with a handful of Balm,
as much Mint and unſet Hyſop, half
a pound of Dates, as many Figs, and
one pound of Raiſons of the Sun ;
diſtil all together, and let it be the
conſtant Drink in a Conſumption.

A good Milk-Water *for* Surfeit *or* Worms.

TAKE of Rue, Wormwood, Carduus and Mint, each three handfuls ; cut the Herbs and ſteep them
all

all Night in two quarts of Milk; diftil
it off next Morning in a cold Still;
from this Quantity draw three pints,
then diftil this Water over again, with
the fame quantity of Milk and Herbs;
fweeten it to your Tafte, if for Children; but for wifer People, 'tis beft
alone,

Strong Elder-berry-Water.

TAKE a Bufhel of Elder-berries, and
put to them a quart of Ale-yeaft,
let them ftand nine or ten Days, ftirring it two or three times a Day, and
then diftil it in a Limbeck: 'Tis a very
good Cordial in any Illnefs.

A Cordial Mint-Water.

TAKE one pound of Mint, ftript
from the Stalks, and gather'd the
Day before you weigh it; a quarter
of a pound of Liquorifh, thin flic'd,
one ounce of Anifeeds, one ounce of
Carraway-

Carraway-ſeeds, one pound of Raiſons
of the Sun ſton'd, ſteep theſe together
in a gallon of good ſtrong Claret ; diſtil
it off a Limbeck, or cold Still if you
don't like it ſo hot and ſtrong ; let it
drop on a little fine Sugar, through a
Bag of Saffron.

A good Milk-Water.

TAKE one pound of Carduus, half
a pound of Wormwood, Spear-
mint, Balm ſhred a little ; put them
in an ordinary Still, with a gallon of
Milk ; and diſtil it off leiſurely : 'Tis
good in any Thirſt.

Another Milk-Water.

CARDUUS and Wormwood, of
each one handful, Spear-mint two
handfuls, pick and cut the Herbs, and
pour upon them a pint of Sack ; let
them ſtand all Night and next Day,
put them into a cold Still, with a gallon

lon of new Milk, or new Whey Clarified : Draw off while it runs good.

A most excellent Drink for the King's-Evil in the Eyes.

TAKE Sage, Celandine, Yarrow, Bitany, three Leav'd Grafs, Cinqfoile, Daify-roots and Leaves, of each a handful, Honey-fuckles and Ground-Ivy, the fame quantity; pick, wafh, dry, and bruife them, and put to them a good quart of White-wine, or Beer, fteep them two Nights and Days; prefs the Herbs out, and Drink four fpoonfuls Morning and Night : Juft as you Drink it, fqueeze in the Juice of fifty Millepedes, frefh bruis'd, --

---

A good Scar-Cloth.

TAKE one pint of Oil of Olives, eight ounces of Red-Lead, Virgins-wax four ounces; of Ointment of Populion, Oil of Rofes, and Oil of Camo-

Camomile, of each one ounce; ſet the pint of Oil on the Fire, and melt the Wax in it; then put in the Populion, and other Oils; when all is melted, put in the Red-Lead, ſtir all well together, and let them boil 'till they are Black; then dip in your Cloth.

An Incomparable Salve *for the Eyes.*

TAKE two ounces of *May* Butter, one ounce of Virgins-wax, half an ounce of Camphire, one ounce of Powder of Tutty; you muſt firſt put your Wax and Camphire, into a Silver Porringer, and let both melt on a gentle ſlow Fire together; conſtantly ſtirring 'till they be diſſolved, ſome little time after put in your *May* Butter, and diſſolve it with a large ſpoonful of Red Roſe-Water; keep it on the Fire till all be incorporated; then add the Powder of Tutty, and mix all very well; take it from the Air; and when you lie to Sleep, gently anoint your Eye-lid with it.

The

The Smallage-Ointment.

TAKE a handful of Smallage, as much Mallows, and as much Elder; pick and fhred all fmall; put them into a Skillet, with a pound of Mutton-fuet fhred fmall; let all boil together: Strain it, and keep it to anoint any Swelling.

A very good Plaifter *for a Stomach Sore with Coughing.*

TAKE of *Burgundy*-Pitch, Rofin, and Bees-wax, of each one ounce; melt thefe together: Then take three-quarters of an ounce of coarfe Turpentine, and half an ounce of Oyl of Mace; melt thefe with the other, and keep it for Ufe: When you have Occafion, fpread it on Sheep's-leather prick'd full of Holes; and when you lay it on, grate fome Nutmeg over it.

To

To give certain Eaſe in the Tooth-ach.

TAKE *French*-Flies, Methridate, and a few drops of Vinegar; beat this to a Paſte, and lay a Plaiſter on the Cheek-bone, or behind the Ear: 'Twill Bliſter, but rarely fails to Cure.

Plaiſters *for a* Fever.

BEAT two handfuls of Rue, with as many Currants, 'till they are fine, and well mix'd; ſpread it on Cloths, and bind it to the Wriſts, and Soles of the Feet: This draws from the Head; and if laid on in time, does as much good as Pigeons to the Feet, in Extremity.

An

An Ointment *that is good for any* Ach *or* Swelling *in Man or Beaſt.*

TAKE of unſet Hyſſop, Goats-Rue, Adder-ſpear, Alehoof, Wormwood, Camomile, Ladies-mantle, Plantain, Harts-tongue, Ladder to Heaven, Southernwood, Red-Sage, Agrimony, Bone-wort, Amber-leaves, Bay-leaves, of each one handful; ſhred theſe, and ſtamp them together: Then mix with them one pound and a half of Butter without Salt, and make it up in nine Balls, and let it lie nine Days; then boil it over the Fire gently: When it looks very Green, ſtrain it off, and keep it for Uſe.

This Number of Days, and Balls, ſeems ſuperſtitious and whimſical; but it has been ſo long approv'd in the Family from whence I had it, that I cannot doubt of its Virtues, tho' I ſmile at the Preparation.

An

An Ointment *for a* Burn.

TAKE of Houfleek, fmooth Plan-
tain-leaves, and green Elder, each
one pound ; ftamp them together fmall;
put to them a quarter of a pint of Wine-
Vinegar, three fpoonfuls of Urine, and
four ounces of Old Tallow-Candle, with
three pints of Oyl-Olive; boil thefe two
or three Hours, ftirring them conftantly with a Stick: Then ftrain it
through a new Canvas-Strainer, and
put it on the Fire again, with four
ounces of Yellow Bees-wax fliced thin ;
let it boil half an Hour this time, and
pour it into Pots. 'Twill keep many
Years, if ty'd down with Bladders.
When you ufe it, rub White Paper 'till
'tis foft, then fpread it over with the
Ointment, and anoint the Burn with
the Ointment: Do it with a Feather,
and lay the Paper over it : Do this
Morning and Night, 'till 'tis quite Well.
'Twill Skin the Wound, as well as take
out the Fire; therefore be fure to ufe
nothing elfe : 'Twill give Eafe in a
quarter of an Hour. 'Tis a certain
as well

as well as a quick Cure, if the Vitals are not burn'd; and is recommended, on the Experience of a Person of great Worth and Charity. A third-part of this Quantity will laft many Years, and may be made very Cheap.

An Ointment *which is a certain Cure for any* Scabs, Pimples, *or Old Inveterate* Itch.

TAKE a quarter of an ounce of Red Precipitate, grind it on a Marble-ftone 'till 'tis as fine as the Flower of Brimftone; mix this with an ounce of Flower of Brimftone, and work both up with three ounces of Butter without Salt, as it comes from the Churn; mix it very well, and anoint the Place very thin with the Ointment. 'Tis not the Nature of it to Check, but Draw Out the Diftemper; and in a Week or Ten Days Confinement, will make an abfolute Cure.

I fhould fay many things to recommend this, being fure of its Virtues; but

but it will not need that, to Any-body
of Judgment.

A very Good Poultis *for a* Sore-
Breaft, *to Break it, if there
be Occafion* ; *and alfo Heal
it, without any other Salve.*

TAKE of Smallage, Spear-mint,
and Wormwood, each a good
handful ; boil all thefe in Milk, and
thicken it with Oat-meal : Lay it on
as Hot as you can bear it, and repeat
it when Hard or Dry.

An Incomparable Ointment *for
a* Strain, Weaknefs *or* Shrink-
ing *in the* Nerves.

TAKE Sweet-marjoram, Penny-
royal, Rofemary-tops, Camomil-
flowers, Lavender-flowers, Sage, and
young Bay-leaves, of each a large handful ; a very large Nutmeg, and its
weight

weight in Mace; the Rind of four Lemons, and as many Oranges: Stamp
all very fine, and boil it in a quarter
of a pint of rich *Malaga*-Wine, and
half a pound of unsalted Butter: Let it
boil 'till the Wine is wasted; press it
through a fine Sieve, and keep it cool
for Use. Rub it Morning and Night
before the Fire, on the Part affected.

The French-King's Balsom.

TAKE Red-Sage, and Rue, of
each half a pound; young Bay-
leaves, and Wormwood, of each a
quarter of a pound: Stamp them
unwash'd in a Mortar, with a pound
and a half of Sheep's-suet hot from the
Sheep, 'till 'tis all of a Colour: Then
add to it a quart of Oyl-Olive, and work
that with the rest: Then put it into an
Earthen Pot well stopt for eight Days:
Then boil it on a soft Fire: Being
ready to take off, pour in three ounces
of Oyl of Spike; let it boil a little together; then strain it, and keep it for
Use: Take care it do not burn. It
must

muſt be made in *May*, and will keep many Years: Rub'd into the ſmall of the Back, it eaſes the Stone: The quantity of half a Pea in the Ear, chafed in and ſtopt with black Wool, helps Pains there; It Cures Stiffneſs or Streins, in Man or Beaſt; as alſo Bruiſes, Over-ſtretching of Veins, Fellons, Anguiſh, or Swelling of Wounds: It eaſes the Cramp; and is a good and uſeful Balſom in all Families.

For the Biting of a Mad-Dog.

TAKE four ounces of Rue, four ounces of *London* Treacle, four ſpoonfuls of ſcrap'd Pewter, and four ounces of Garlick; ſtamp the Garlick, and boil all in a pottle of Stale ſtrong Ale; ſtrain this Drink; let that which is thick be apply'd to the Wound, and take nine ſpoonfuls of the clear, for nine Days together.

An

An Ointment *for a Child that has the Rickets.*

TAKE one ounce of Beef Marrow, as much Oil of Lillies, and Tamarisk, Bees-wax two ounces, Gum Amoniacum diffolv'd in Vinegar, half an ounce; Juice of Briany-roots, Smallage, and Golden-Rod, of each one ounce; let all boil, 'till the Juice of the Herbs be confumed: With this anoint the Belly of the Child, rubbing it in with your warm Hand by the Fire, half an Hour every Night. 'Tis good if the Belly is Swell'd with Rickets, Worms, or Ague.

An Ointment, *for the Back of a Weak Ricketty Child.*

PICK Snails clean out of the Shells, and prick them full of Holes, hang them up in a Cloth, and put a Bafon to catch what drops from them; which you muft boil up with Speracity, and blades of Mace, of each one ounce:
Rub

Rub this Ointment along the Back-bone, round the Neck, Wriſts and Ancles. Uſe this conſtantly Night and Morning, and chafe it in by the Fire ; this, with the Drink that follows, has Recover'd many Weak Children from Sickneſs, Lameneſs, and Deformity.

The Ricketty *Drink.*

PUT an ounce of Rhubarb, three hundred live Wood-lice, Saſſafras, China, and Eringo-roots, of each three ounces ; Roots of Oſmond-royal, two onnces ; Raiſons of the Sun ſton'd, two ounces ; Hart's-Tongue, two handfuls ; Put theſe into ſix quarts of Small Ale, and Drink Spring and Fall no other Drink. 'Tis almoſt infallible for weak Children.

A cooling Drink in a Fever *or* Plurifie.

PUT an ounce of Pearl-Barley, into three pints of Water, ſhift it twice ; beat half an ounce of Almonds, with a

bit

bit of Lemon-peel, and a fpoonful or two of the Water; when they are very fine, wafh the Almond-Milk through your Sieve, with three pints of Barley-Water; in the laft boiling of this, you may put Mellon-feeds, and Pumpion-feeds, of each half an ounce; white Poppey-feeds, half a dram; when thefe are well boil'd, mix the Liquor with the Almonds, and ftrain all. Sweeten it with Syrop of Lemons, for a Fever, or Syrop of Maiden-hair, and Drink four ounces every three or four Hours.

Another Drink *in a* Fever.

TAKE a little Sage, a little Balm, and a little Wood-forrel, wafh and dry them; flice a fmall Lemon, (after you have par'd it clean from the white and bitter part;) To thefe Herbs and fliced Lemon, pour three pints of boiling Water: Sweeten it to your Tafte, and Drink as freely as you pleafe.

Another

Another Drink.

TO three pints of Barley-Water, often ſhifted, put Harts-horn, and Ivory-ſhavings, of each three drams; Quick-graſs-Roots, two ounces; Currants, one ounce; Red-roſe-Water, half a pint; a very little Balm : Let it boil and ſweeten it with Syrop of Lemons or Violets. If the Patient is Coſtive, a few drops of Spirit of Vitriol ſerves inſtead of Lemons, when that cannot be had : Of this you may Drink freely in a Fever or Quinſie.

Another Sort.

CLEAR Poſſet-Drink, pour'd on Wood-ſorrel only, is good, and allays Thirſt better than any other; and Pippins ſlic'd into Milk, is as good and better than all; if you have a Lemon to ſlice in with them, being not ſharp enough of themſelves, to turn it to a pleaſant clearneſs.

A

A cold Caudle *in a* Fever.

BOIL a quart of Spring-water, let it stand 'till cold, then add the Yolk of one Egg, the Juice of a small Lemon, six spoonfuls of Sack, and Sugar to your Taste; Syrop of Lemons one ounce, if you have not fresh Lemons, does as well; Brew all together 'till well mixt, then Drink freely.

Elder-flower-Water cold still'd, is an excellent Drink for Heat and Thirst; quicken each draught with five or six drops of Spirit of Vitriol; and sweeten it to your Taste.

Wall-nut-Water, *good in* Agues *or* Fever.

TAKE a pound of Rue, and a pound of Green Wall-nuts, before the Shell be hard, a pound of good Figs; bruise all and distil it: Take a Draught before your Fit, and try to Sweat after it.

An

An excellent Snail-Water *in a* Conſumption.

TAKE a peck of large Shell Snails, lay them on a hot Hearth before the Fire; let them lie 'till they have done Hiſſing and Spitting; then wipe them from the Froth, and break them in a Mortar; have a quart of Earth-Worms, ſlit and ſcoured clean with Salt and Water; beat them with the Snails; then take Angelica, Salendine, Wood-ſorrel, Agrimony, Bearfoot, Barberry-bark, Great Dock-roots, of each two handfuls; Rue half a handful, Roſemary-flowers, one quart; half a pound of Harts-horn, Termarick, and Fenigreek, of each two ounces; half an ounce of powder'd Saffron, and three ounces of Cloves freſh beat; ſhred theſe Ingredients, and Infuſe all in three gallons of Strong Ale, for twelve Hours; then diſtil it, and draw off what runs good; and take three ſpoonfuls of this in a Glaſs of Sack, or White-wine, an Hour before every Meal. Uſe moderate Exerciſe with it. 'Tis high-

ly

ly recommended, and has been us'd with conſtant Succeſs in Conſumptions and Jaundice.

A Posset-Drink, to be taken before the fit of an Ague.

POUR a gallon of clear Posset-Drink, upon four large handfuls of Angelica; shred small, let it infuse, 'till 'tis very strong: Let the Person, if possible, Drink all, that the Stomach may be perfectly clear; and go into a warm Bed, as soon as the Vomit has done working: Cover yourself close, and try to sweat. It has seldom fail'd, and is a safe Vomit.

A good Epidemick-Water.

TAKE Rue, Roſemary, Pimpernel, Roſaſolis, Balm, Scordium, Carduus, Dragon, Marigold-flowers and Leaves, Goats-Rue, Mint, and Angelica, of each two handfuls; take

the

the Roots of Elecampane, Piony, Ma-
ſterwort, and Butter-bur, of each one
pound ; Gentian, Tormentil, Scorzone-
ra, and *Virginia*-Snake-weed, of each
four ounces ; Saffron one ounce : Infuſe all theſe, when ſhred, in two
quarts of White-wine, one quart of
Water, and one quart of *French*-Bran-
dy diſtil'd, and uſe it in any Malignant
Diſtemper.

An admirable Poſſet-Drink, in a Pluriſie, or Shortneſs of Breath.

INFUSE two ounces of Flax-feed,
in a pint of clear Poſſet-Drink ; firſt
bruiſe the Seeds. Drink this quantity at a Draught every Morning, and
at Night, if very Ill.

It has the ſame Virtues of Linſeed-
Oil ; but is not ſo hard to take.

For

For an Inflammation in the Throat.

INFUSE one large handful of Cinqfoile in a quart of Water, let it boil to a pint; strain it, and sweeten it with Honey very sweet, and swallow two or three spoonfuls often. This, tho' a simple Medicine, has done great Cures, and may be rely'd on. The Herb is otherwise call'd *Five-leav'd-Grass.*

For a Cough, *and* Shortness of Breath.

TAKE eight ounces of Colts-foot pick'd clean from the Stalks; beat it to a pefect Conferve, with four ounces of Brown Sugar-candy, four ounces of Raisons stoned: When 'tis very fine, and well mix'd, add four ounces of Conferve of Roses; then add twenty drops of Spirit of Sulphur, and ten drops of Spirit of Vitriol: Mix it well, and

and take as much as a large Nutmeg, as often as you pleafe. I think the Juice of the Colts-foot, mixt with the Sugar-candy, is better than the Leaves, without ftraining.

A good Way to make Caudle.

TO four full-quarts of Water you may put a pint of Whole Oat-meal; let it boil very flow for five or fix Hours at leaft; then ftrain it out, and put to two quarts three large blades of Mace, a full pint and a half of White or Rhenifh-wine; and make it fweet to your Tafte; And juft as you take it off the Fire, flice in a Lemon from which all the White is cut, which is apt, by lying long, to make it bitter; juft the Yellow of the Peel may be put in. A little Salt does very well in Caudle, but is not often ufed.

A very

A very Good Purge *in a* Fever.

TAKE Sena two drams, Rhubarb one dram, Tamarinds two drams; boil thefe in half a pint of Water, 'till two-thirds is wafted: To what remains, add half an ounce of Cream of Tartar fweetned with one ounce of Syrop of Succory, or Syrop of Rofes folutive; ftrain and drink it at a Draught. In the Working, drink Clarify'd Whey, rather than Poffet-Drink. 'Tis good to Cool and Thin the Blood.

An Incomparable Drink *in a Thirfty* Fever.

AN ounce an a half of Tamarinds, three ounces of Currants, and two ounces of fton'd Raifons, boiled in three pints of Water 'till near one-third be confumed. Strain and drink this when you are Coftive.

A Draught

A Draught *for a* Conſumption.

TAKE Mint, and Red Roſe-water, of each two large ſpoonfuls, Sugar-candy finely beat one ounce; warm theſe together, with a little grated Nutmeg; pour to it near half a pint of Milk juſt warm from the Cow. Drink this twice a Day, for ſix Weeks, in the Spring. It has recover'd many from Weakneſs, and Faint Sweats.

An Excellent Electuary *for a* Conſumption.

TAKE Hore-hound, Harts-tongue, Liver-wort, Maiden-hair, Egrimony, Unſet Hyſſop, Germander, and Colts-foot, of each one handful; boil them in a gallon of Spring-water 'till half be conſumed : Then take three pounds of Live Honey, half an ounce of Powder of Elecampane, and an ounce of Powder of Annis-ſeed ; ſift them both through a Sieve : Boil theſe together 'till it come to the Conſiſtence of an Electuary. Take the quantity of a
Nutmeg

Nutmeg fasting in the Morning, and fast an Hour after it. Take the like quantity at Night when you go to Bed.

A Poppy-Water *for* Surfeits.

BREW ten gallons of Strong Ale-Wort; when 'tis cool, work it with Yeast, and add as many fresh Red Poppies as the Wort will conveniently wet, so that you may stir it daily : Let the Poppies Infuse in this Wort three Days and Nights; then draw it off in a Limbeck as quick as you can, 'till the whole is distill'd off : Mix the Small and Strong together, and take a glass at any time, with or without Sugar, after a full or disgusting Meal. 'Tis not much stronger than a Simple Water, but has been the only Cordial of an Infirm Lady, who has us'd it ever since Fifteen, and she is now Ninety-seven. This of my own knowledge.

Another

Another for a Surfeit.

BOIL a handful of frefh or dry'd Poppies in Ale, with an ounce of Carraway-feeds bruifed: Sweeten it, and drink a large Draught. If the Stomach is fo fick as to difcharge it, repeat it 'till it does ftay, and Sleep on it.

A Rich Surfeit Cordial-Water.

TAKE four pound of frefh Red Poppies, Infufe them in four quarts of Brandy; add to it half a pound of Dates fliced, half a pound of Figs fliced, a pound of Raifons ftoned; Carraway and Angelica-feeds bruifed, of each one ounce; Mace, Cinamon, Cloves, and Nutmeg, of each a quarter of an ounce; Marigold-flowers, and Balm, of each one handful; Sugarcandy one pound; Hot Angelica and Cold, of each one pint: Steep all thefe a Month, ftirring them every Day. If you have a convenient Place, let it ftand in the Sun.

A Whol-

A Wholsome Cordial.

TAKE one pound of Gentian-roots sliced, common Dock-roots sliced half a pound; Centory, both Flowers and Leaves, of each half a pound: Put these into a great Glass, with one pound of Poppies: Pour upon these Ingredients six quarts of White-wine: Let it stand twenty-four Hours to Infuse; then draw it off in a Limbeck. 'Tis Good and Safe in any Illness of the Stomach.

For the Gout.

MAKE a Conserve of Buck-bean, with the weight in Sugar-candy; beat both fine, and take as much as a large Nutmeg, first and last; and drink a Tea made of the same Herb every Morning and Afternoon, constantly, for one whole Year.

This alone, without any other Medicine, made a perfect Cure in a Person that had been many Years most grievously

grievouſly afflicted; and is effectual in
the *Scurvy*, or *Rheumatick Pains.* Where
the Patient is Weak, and very Reſtleſs,
'tis beſt to mix a third-part *Venice*-
Treacle in the Conſerve they take
when going to Reſt.

A Drink *for the* Gout.

SArſaparilla eight ounces, Saſſafras,
China, and Harts-horn-Shavings,
of each three ounces, Angelica-Roots
three ounces, Raiſons one pound, and
the Roots of Sweet-ſmelling-Flag three
ounces, of Candy'd Eringo-root half a
pound; hang theſe in ſix gallons of
ſmall Ale, when you Tun it up: And
as ſoon as 'tis a Fortnight old, drink
of it conſtantly.

'Tis an Incomparable *Drink* to
Sweeten the Blood, and Correct thoſe
very Sharp Humours that occaſion
that diſmal Tormenting Diſtemper.

N   *For*

For *the* Head-ach.

DRY Rofemary before the Fire 'till 'twill crumble to a very fine Powder, one pugil of Saffron ; and with the Powder of Rofemary and Saffron make the Yolk of an Egg into a ftiff Poultis, and lay it as hot as you can endure it to the Temples.

For *the* Stone *and* Gravel.

TAKE of Caffia newly drawn one ounce and a half, choice Rhubard in Powder a dram and a half, *Cyprus-*Turpentine well wafhed feven drams, Spic'd Diatragacanth one fcruple, Powder of Licorice half a dram ; mix it in a good quantity of Syrop of Marfh-mallows. Take the quantity of a Wall-nut in a Morning fafting : Drink a Draught of plain Ale-Poffet-drink immediately after it ; then Walk an Hour : And after that, drink a pint (if your Stomach will bear it) of White-

White-wine-Poſſet ſweeten'd with Syrop of Marſh-mallows.

N. B. This was the Preſcription of a Learned Phyſician ; and has been long kept as a choice Secret in a very Charitable Family, who have made numberleſs Experiments of it with miraculous Succeſs, even to Diſſolve the Stone.

Another for Stoppage of Water, *in the* Stone.

TAKE four ſpoonfuls of the Juice of Parſley in a pint of White-wine ; ſweeten it with Syrop of Marſh-mallows, and (if you can) drink the whole quantity at a Draught.

For the Stone.

MAKE a very ſtrong Decoction of Mallows, thus ; Put in half a peck of Leaves into one gallon of Water ; let it boil to near half the quantity : Then ſtrain it, and add half as many Leaves, and boil it again : Then add Licorice, ſtoned Raiſons, and Syrop

of

of Marſh-mallows, of each two ounces; and drink continually of this Drink: It has given Eaſe to many in Extremity. Obſerve to ſtrain it clean, and let it ſettle from the Thick before you pour it off.

For *the* Stone.

TAKE of good White-wine one pint; Fennel, and Parſley-water, of each one pint: Into this Mixture put one ounce of Live Wood-lice well cleanſed, one Lemon ſliced thin, and two ounces of Syrop of Marſh-mallows; put theſe into a Jug to Infuſe for five or ſix Days: Then ſtrain it out, and let the Patient take four ounces at a time, twice a Day.

For *the* Scurvy.

TAKE Scurvy-graſs, Garden-Tanſy, Wood-ſorrel, and Golden-rod, of each one handful; beat theſe Herbs to a Conſerve with their weight in Sugar; add to them an ounce of Powder

der of Wake-Robin: Take as much Syrop of Oranges as will make this into an Electuary, of which take a dram three times a Day, for fix Weeks together, in the Spring; drinking after it the following *Drink*.

TAKE Garden-Tanfy, Garden-Scurvy-grafs, of each fix handfuls; Buck-bean, Water-creffes, Brook-lime, and Wood-forrel, of each four handfuls, the Peel of fix Oranges, and one ounce of Nutmegs bruifed; Infufe thefe in two gallons of New Strong Ale-wort; let it work together a Day and a Night; then diftil it off in a Cold Still as long as it runs Good: Mix the Small, and drink a Wine-Glafs-full after every Dofe of the *Electuary.*

This has been taken with great Succefs, by People who have been much afflicted with *Scurvy Pains*, and *Spots.* It has, by conftant Taking, Cur'd a *Rhumatifm.*

For

For the same.

ONE handful of Garden-Tanſy, as much Sage, and twice as much Scurvy-graſs, ſteep'd in two quarts of White-wine, or Strong Ale. Drink half a pint of this Morning and Night.

For the same.

INTO five gallons of well Brew'd Small Ale, put in a Bag One large handful of Fir-tree-Tops cut ſmall, two handfuls of Scurvy-graſs, as much Water-creſſes, one pound of Burdock-root ſcraped and ſliced, the Juice and Rinds of twelve *Sevil*-Oranges; let theſe be put in while the Ale is Work-ing: When it has done, ſtop it down 'till 'tis Fine; then drink of it for a Month, or Six Weeks.

Uſe the ſame for a *Dropſy*; adding only a quarter of a pound of Muſtard-ſeed, and half a pound of Horſe-radiſh-root.

An

An Excellent Purging-Ale *for* a Dropſy.

SENA four ounces, Saſſafras, and Tartar, of each two ounces; Jalop, and Licorice, of each one ounce; Rhubarb, Coriander, and Annis-ſeed, of each one ounce; Polypodiam eight ounces, Broom-aſhes one quart, and one ounce of Cloves; put all in a Bag, with ſome little Weight to ſink it: Take Scabious, and Agrimony, of each three handfuls; of the Roots of Daneswort one handful, Raiſons of the Sun ſtoned one pound, with a little Ginger: Put theſe Ingredients into ſweet Alewort when you put in your Hops, and let all boil together half an Hour; then pour it ſcalding-hot on your Bag of Drugs: When 'tis cold enough, ſet it to Work with Yeaſt: When it has done Working, ſtop it up for Twelve Days, or a Fortnight: Hang the Bag of Drugs in the Veſſel. Drink a large Glaſs of this in the Morning, and at Four in the Afternoon, unleſs you find it Works too much at firſt; if ſo, leſſen

your

your Dofe; but take it Daily, 'till you have taken all.

For a Dropfy.

TAKE Broom, and burn it by it-felf, in a clean Oven; fift the Afhes from the Stalks and Coals that are not quite confumed, and put two full pounds of thefe Afhes into a two-quart Bottle; pour on old Hock, 'till the Bottle is up to the neck; take care 'tis not too full; if it has not room to ferment, 'twill be apt to fplit the Bot-tle: digeft it in hot Afhes by the Fire, or in the Sun, and fhake it often: when it has ftood three or four Days, pour off a quart of the clear Lye: if it is not perfectly fine, decant again and again, 'till it is fo: fill up your Bottle a-gain with Hock, and do as before, 'till all the ftrength of the Afhes be out. Drink this firft, and at four or five in the Afternoon; continue it for fome time, and 'twill carry off the Dropfical Humour: While you take it, let the Meat you Eat be dry roafted; and your Drink, ftrong Ale or Wine,

For

For the Dropſy.

MIX four ounces of Syrop of Elder-berries, with two ounces of Oil of Turpentine, incorporate them well to-gether; and take one large ſpoonful of this mixture, firſt and laſt, for a Fort-night.

Note, That Sea-bisket, and New Raiſons of the Sun (if they can be had) eaten conſtantly, inſtead of Sup-pers, have Cured that Diſtemper with-out Phyſick: Eſpecially if the Party can refrain from ſmall Liquors.

For the Jaundice.

CUT off the top of a *Sevil*-Orange, and take out as well as you can the middle Core and Seeds, without the Juice; fill the vacancy with Saf-fron, and lay the top on again; then roaſt it carefully without burning, and throw it into a pint of White-wine: Drink a quarter of a pint Faſting, for

nine

nine Days; it greatly fweetens and clears the Blood.

To Sweeten the Blood, in Scurvy, Jaundice, or any Pains in the Limbs.

TAKE Scurvy-grafs, Maiden-hair, Wild Germander, Wood-forrel, Fumitory, of each half a handful; Wild Mercury one handful, Damask-Rofes two handfuls; put thefe into two quarts of clarify'd Whey; let all ftand 'till 'tis fcalding hot, then ftrain it off; and Drink half a pint at a Draught, four or five times in a Day, for a Month or five Weeks in the Spring. This is highly recommended in the Gout.

A good Bitter Wine.

TAKE two quarts of ftrong White-wine, Infufe in it one dram of Rhubarb, a dram and half of Gentian-root, Roman Wormwood, tops of Carduus, Centory,

Centory, Camomile-flowers, of each three drams, Yellow peep of Oranges, half an ounce; Nutmegs, Mace, and Cloves, of each one dram: Infufe all thefe two Days and Nights; ftrain and Drink a glafs Fafting, and an Hour before Dinner, and Supper: Add Filings of Steel (if 'tis proper) two ounces.

A Pleafant and Safe Medicine, *for the* Yellow Jaundice.

ROAST a large Lemon 'till 'tis foft, take care it do not break; cut it and fqueeze it (while 'tis very hot) upon a dram of Termerick flic'd or grated, and half a dram of Saffron; pour upon thefe Ingredients a pint of good White-wine: Let all Infufe one Night; and in the Morning, Fafting, take a quarter of a pint of this Liquor; fweeten it to your Tafte with Sugar-candy; or if your Stomach can bear it, the Sugar-candy may be omitted; repeat this for four Mornings, or longer if you have Occafion. 'Tis for the moft part a certain cure.

For

For the Stone.

WASH, dry, and very finely Powder the inner Skin of Pigeons-Gizzards: Take as much as will lie on a Shilling of this Powder, in a glaſs of White-wine. This does very often give eaſe in wracking Pain.

Another for the Stone.

DRY and Powder the Haw-thorn-Berries, and take as much as will lie on a Shilling in a glaſs of White-wine: This has done great Cures, by conſtant taking; it may be taken in Ale, if you cannot have Wine; the Virtue is in the Berry, and has been experienc'd to the great eaſe of many poor People, in Ale as well as Wine; but the laſt is beſt: And a Poſſet-Drink turn'd with White-wine, is a proper Vehicle for it. Take it Faſting, or when in Pain.

An-

An excellent Drink *in the* Gout *or* Rhumatiſm.

TAKE ſix ounces of Saſſafras; Sarſaparilla, and China, of each four ounces; Liquoriſh and Aniſeeds, of each two ounces; Sage of Virtue, half a handful; Candy'd Eringo-root, two ounces; Raiſons and Figs, of each half a pound: Put all theſe into four quarts of Water: let it infuſe over a ſlow Fire, 'till one third is waſted. Strain and Drink it conſtantly, to ſweeten the Blood.

A good Mouth-Water, *to be us'd Daily in the* Scurvy.

TAKE half a handful of Red-roſe-Leaves, three ounces of Black-thorn-Bark ſlic'd, a bit of Allum; boil theſe in a pint of Claret, and as much Water, 'till a third is waſted; then put in the peel of one *Sevil*-Orange, a handful of Scurvy-graſs, and as much Powder'd

der'd Myrrh as will lie on a Shilling; ftir all together, and let it boil up; then ftrain it, and hold a Mouthful as long as you can, once or twice a Day: It faftens loofe Teeth, and makes the Gums grow up to the Teeth.

A Gargle *for a* Sore Throat.

TAKE Plantain, and Red-rofe-Water, of each half a pint; the Whites of Eggs beat into Water, four fpoonfuls; Juice of Houfe-leek, frefh beat, four fpoonfuls; as much of the Water in which Jews-Ears have been boil'd; twenty drops of Spirit of Vitriol, and an ounce of Honey of Rofes.

For a Canker *in the* Mouth *or* Gums.

MIX forty drops of Spirit of Vitriol, in an ounce of Honey of Rofes: Keep the Sore Place always moift with this mixture; and 'tis a certain Cure.

A

A Gargle *in the* Palſey.

PUT a large ſpoonful of Muſtard-ſeed, bruis'd, into a pint of White-wine; drop in Spirit of Vitriol, to make it ſharp; and waſh your Mouth often in a Day, hold it as long at the root of your Tongue, as you can endure it at a time.

Another Gargle *in the* Palſey.

POUR a quart of boiling Water upon a very large handful of La-vender-flowers; let it Infuſe in the Aſhes, 'till 'tis very ſtrong; ſtrain it, and add a ſpoonful of Vinegar, a ſpoon-ful of Hungary-Water, and a ſpoonful of Honey. Waſh your Mouth often with this; it is a very good Gargle.

A

A constant Daily Wash *for your* Teeth.

TO one quart of Claret, put an ounce of Bole-armoniac, half an ounce of Myrrh, one dram of Allum ; Salt of Vitriol, ten grains; an ounce of Hungary-Water, and two ounces of Honey of Roses ; when these have stood in a warm Sun, or near the Fire for three Days, set it by to settle; and pour a spoonful of it into a Tea-cup of Water, with which wash your Teeth: It preserves them Sound, and makes them White.

To clean very foul Spotted Teeth.

MAKE a Skewer very sharp at one end, over which wind a bit of fine Rag, tie it on very hard, and cut it very sharp, that it may be like a fine Pencil for Painting; dip this in Spirit of Salt, take it out immediately, and dip it then into a Cup of fair Water,

in

in which hold it for a Moment; with
this Rag, so carefully wet, Rub your
Teeth, and take care you do not touch
your Lips or Gums; have a cup of
cold Water ready to wash your Mouth,
that the Rag has not been dip'd in:
With this you may make any furr'd
Teeth as White as Snow; but you
must not use it often or carelesly.
When they are once thus clean'd, the
Claret-Wash will preserve them so.

A Mucilage *in a* Sore Throat.

TAKE four drams of Quince-seed,
decoct it in a quarter of a pint
of Rose or Plantain-Water, 'till 'tis a
strong Jelly; add a spoonful of the
White of an Egg beat to Water; and
sweeten it with Syrop of Mulberries,
or Rasberries.

O *To*

To Cure a Cough *and* Shortnefs of Breath.

TAKE Elecampane-roots, and boil them very tender and pulp them fine through a Sieve, take their weight in the pulp of codl'd Pippins; if you have a pound weight of both together, boil it in a pint and half of clarify'd Honey, for half an Hour; then take one ounce of Powder of Licorice, and as much Powder of Anifeeds; mix all well together, and take a dram Morning and Night, and in the Afternoon: 'Tis an excellent Medicine in an Afthma.

Another for a Cough.

ROAST a large Lemon very carefully without burning; when 'tis thorough hot, cut and fqueeze it into a cup, upon three ounces of Sugarcandy finely Powder'd; take a fpoonful whenever your Cough troubles you: 'Tis as good as 'tis pleafant.

For

For the same.

TAKE two ounces of Syrop of Poppies, as much Conserve of Red Roses; mix and take one spoonful for Three Nights, when going to Rest.

For the same, with a Hoarsness.

SYROP of Jujubes and Althea, of each two Ounces, Lohoch Sanans one ounce; Saffron and Water-flag powder'd, of each a scruple: Lick it off a Licorice-stick when you Cough.

For a Hoarsness.

TAKE every Night, going to Rest, half a pint of Mum, as warm as you can drink it at a Draught, for three Nights together.

For a Hooping-Cough, very Good.

TAKE a quart of Spring-water, put to it a large handful of Chincups that grow upon Moss, a large

hand.

handful of Unfet Hyffop; boil it to a
pint; ftrain it off, and fweeten it with
Sugar-candy. Let the Child, as oft as
it Coughs, take two fpoonfuls at a
time, if it can.

For a Cough.

MAKE a ftrong Tea of Ale-hoof,
fweeten it with Sugar-candy, and
drink it Firft and Laft.

For a Confumptive Cough.

TAKE half a pound of double-
refin'd Sugar finely beat and fifted,
wet this with Orange-flower-Water,
and boil it up to a Candy-height;
then ftir in an ounce of Caffia-Earth
finely powder'd. If you love Perfume,
a grain of Ambergreefe does well;
drop it in little Cakes on a Mazareen
that has been Butter'd, and wiped.

This has Cured thofe that have
fpit Blood.

A very

A very Good Pectoral Drink *for the ſame.*

TAKE Quitch-graſs-Roots two ounces, Eringo-Roots one ounce, Loris two drams, Harts-horn one ounce, Raiſons ſtoned two ounces, ſix Figs, one ſpoonful of Pearl-Barley, Colts-foot and Sage of Jeruſalem of each one handful; boil theſe in three pints of Water 'till a third-part is waſted; ſtrain it, and diſſolve therein two drams of Sal-prunella, and one ounce of Syrop of Violets. Drink a quarter of a pint often, when you Cough, or are Dry.

Pills *for* Shortneſs of Breath.

TAKE a quarter of an ounce of Powder of Elecampane-root, half an ounce of Powder of Licorice, as much Flower of Brimſtone, and Powder of Annis-ſeed, and two ounces of Sugar-candy powder'd; make all into Pills with a ſufficient quantity of Tar:

Take

Take four large Pills when going to Reft.

This is an Incomparable Medicine for an *Afthma*.

Another for the fame.

HALF a pint of the Juice of Sting-ing Nettles; boil, and fcum it, and mix it up with as much Clarify'd Honey: Take a Spoonful Firft and Laft. It has done mighty Cures.

For an Afthma.

TAKE Hyffop-water, and Poppy-water, of each five ounces; Oxy-mel of Squills three ounces, Syrop of Maiden-hair one ounce: Take One Spoonful when you find any Difficulty of Breathing.

A good Drink *in a* Confumption.

TAKE of St. John's-wort, the Great Daify-flowers (call'd Ox-eyes,) and Scabious, of each two handfuls;

boil

boil thefe in a gallon of Spring-water 'till half be wafted; then ftrain it, and fweeten it with Clarify'd Honey to your Tafte : Take a Quarter of a Pint of this in half a pint of New Milk; make your Liquor juft fo warm; and take it in a Morning, and at Four in the Afternoon.

This *Drink* is highly recommended, and that too upon long Experience.

A Powder *for a* Confumption.

TAKE twelve dozen of the fmalleft Grigs you can get, wipe them very clean; bake them in a well-glaz'd Pan all Night; fet it into the Oven again 'till they are dry enough to Powder; then make them into a very fine Powder, and take as much as will lie on a Half-Crown, three times a Day, drinking with it a glafs of Old Malaga, or Canary.

'Tis Reftorative, and well Approv'd by many who have try'd it with Succefs.

For

For Sweating in the Night, *in a* Consumption.

DRINK a glass of Tent, or Old Malaga, with a Toast, every Morning early, and sleep an Hour after it.

This is good for Consumptive Persons, or such as are Weak, in recovering a long Sickness.

For a Shortness of Breath.

TAKE Flower of Brimstone, and Elecampane-Root finely powder'd, of each an equal quantity; mix this into an Electuary with Clarify'd Honey, and take it whenever you Cough, or find it difficult to Breathe.

For an Asthma; *Incomparable.*

TAKE Juice of Hyssop, Juice of Elecampane-Root, of each one pound; boyl these to a Syrop with
double

double their weight in Honey or Sugar-candy: Take one spoonful of this Syrop, in two spoonfuls of Hyssop-Water, and one spoonful of compound Briany-Water; take this three times a Day.

For a Cough and Shortness of Breath.

TAKE Elecampane-Roots, one ounce; Saffron, a quarter of an ounce; Ground-Ivy and Hyssop, of each one handful; boil this in two quarts of Water, 'till 'tis above half consumed; strain it out, and sweeten it with Sugar-candy, and take three spoonfuls often.

Another for the same.

SYROP of Garlick two spoonfuls, or the Cloves of Garlick preserv'd; either of them very good: But if the Breath be very bad, 'tis best to lose nine or ten ounces of Blood, if the Patient

tient can bear it, before you begin to take so hot a Medicine.

Another for the same.

TAKE one spoonful of Linseed-Oil new drawn, First and Last: This is good in a Plurisie, or any other Cough; and may be used safely at any Age.

For a Chin-Cough.

DRY the Leaves of Box-Tree very well, and Powder them small; and give the Child of this fine Powder, in all its Meat and Drink, that it can be disguised in: 'Tis excellent in that Distemper.

An admirable Electuary *for a* Cough.

TAKE Syrop of Hoar-hound, Ground-Ivy, and White Poppy, of each one ounce; Crabs-eyes, one dram; and Sperma-ceti, half a dram;
mix

mix and beat thefe very fine, and take a little fpoonful when your Cough is troublefome, and at going to Reft.

For the Plurifie.

TAKE Broom-tops, Dandelion, Red Poppies, and Hyffop, of each two handfuls fhred; Flax-feed bruis'd, two ounces; four ounces of frefh Orange-peel, and nine large Balls of frefh Stone-horfe-dung; to thefe Ingredients, put a gallon of Milk, and diftil it in a cold Still: 'Tis an incomparable Water, and may be Drank freely of. If you think it too cold, add a fpoonful of Sack or White-wine, in every glafs.

Another.

MAKE a Poffet-Drink pretty clear, with fmall Ale and White-wine; and to a quart of that, put three balls of Horfe-dung, and one ounce of Angelica-feeds; let it Infufe three Hours; Strain and Drink often, half a pint at a time;

a time : This has the fame Virtue, and is fooner prepared ; but 'tis fo very naufeous, that many Stomachs cannot bear it.

An excellent Water *for the* Stone-Cholick.

PUT four pounds of Haw-berries, bruis'd, into four quarts of ftrong White-wine; let it fteep twenty-four Hours; then draw off, in a cold Still, two quarts of very ftrong; and what runs after, keep by itfelf: A quarter of a pint of the Strongeft, has given Eafe in very bad Fits at once taking ; but if it comes up, you muft repeat it 'till it does ftay.

For

For the Cholick.

SLICE one ounce of the very beft Rhubarb you can get, into a quart of Sack; let it Infufe twelve Hours at leaft, then Drink four large fpoonfuls, and fill your Bottle up again: Drink this Quantity once a Day for fix Weeks or two Months at leaft; when your Rhubarb has loft its virtue, you muft put frefh. This has cured fome People, who could not find Eafe in Opiats, nor the Bath; it muft be conftantly continued, 'till the Bowels and Blood are Strengthened: It has done fuch Miraculous Cures, where even Laudanum could not; that 'tis impoffible to praife it fo much as it deferves.

I do therefore advife every Perfon fo Afflicted, for their own fakes, to make the harmlefs Experiment.

For

For the Cholick.

TAKE a quart of Double-Still'd Aniseed-Water; Infuse in it one ounce of Hirapica; stop it very close, and keep it near a Fire, where it must stand some Days; shake the Glass twice every Day: Take three or four spoon-fuls of this in a Fit, when 'tis New; less will serve, after it has stood a Year or two.

For a Convulsive Cholick.

TAKE Yellow Transparent Amber, grosly Powder'd; Ginger minced; mix and fill a Pipe, Smoke three or four while in Pain, and always going to Rest.

Another for the Cholick.

BOIL four spoonfuls of right good *Irish*-Usquebaugh, in half a pint of Ale, slice in a little Ginger, and sweeten with Syrop of Rhubarb: This is a

pretty

pretty certain Cure, and ſeldom fails to give preſent Eaſe.

For the Cholick.

TAKE the thin Peel that comes off the Kernels of a Ripe Wall-nut dry'd and beat to Powder; the thin Yellow Peel of Orange Powder'd, of each a like Quantity; mix it in a cup of hot Ale and Drink it up. A ſmall ſpoonful of the Powders, mix'd, is a Doſe.

For a Stitch *in the* Side.

TAKE Powder of Angelica-ſeed, and a large Acorn dry'd and powder'd, of each a like quantity: Drink after it a glaſs of Black Cherry-Water.

A

A Poffet-Drink *for a* Cough.

TAKE one handful of Hyffop, four
fprigs of Mint, as much Sa-
voury and Angelica, one handful of
fton'd Raifons, and twelve Figs; Infufe all thefe in three pints of clear
Poffet-Drink; add, when ftrain'd, one
ounce of Syrop of Maiden-hair, as
much Syrop of Violets: Drink often.

To Cure Deafnefs.

TAKE clean fine Black Wool,
and dip it in Civet, put it into the
Ear; as it drys, which in a Day or two
it will, dip it again; and keep it ·
moiften'd in the Ear for three Weeks
or a Month.

Another.

TAKE an equal quantity of good
Hungary-Water, and Oil of Bitter Almonds, beat them together; and
drop

drop three drops in the Ears going to Bed; ſtop them with Black Wool, and repeat this nine Nights at leaſt.

Another for a Pain *in the* Ear.

THE Juice of Mountain Sage, Oil of Fennel, Oil of Bitter Almonds, Oil of Olives; take an equal quantity of each, and mix them well together: Drop into the Pained Ear three drops, for three Nights. 'Twill eaſe and draw out any Impoſthume, if that be the Cauſe.

For a Pain *in the* Ear.

TAKE half a pint of Claret, a quarter of a pint of Wine-Vinegar; put in Sage, Rue, and Roſemary; let it boil up; put it into a New Mug, and hold your Ear cloſe, ſo that the Steam may be ſure to go in: As it cools, heat it again and again; and when the Strength is pretty well waſted, wrap your Head very warm and go into Bed.

P

For

For a *Violent* Cholick-Pain *in the* Side.

MIX an equal quantity of Spirit of Lavender, Spirit of Sal-Armoniac, and *Hungary*-Water; rub it in with a very Hot Hand, and lay a Flannel on as Hot as you can bear it. Repeat this often.

For a Blow or Hurt *in the* Eye.

BEAT the Leaves of Eye-bright with a Rotten Apple; lay it on the Eye as a Poultis: Repeat it as it grows dry. I think the *Juice* of the Eye-bright is beſt.

A Certain Remedy to take Fire out of a Burn.

BEAT an Apple with Sallet-Oyl, 'till 'tis a Poultis pretty ſoft; bind it on the Part; and as it dries, lay on
freſh

freſh. You muſt be ſure to Pare, Core, and Beat your Apple well, for fear of breaking the Skin of the Burn: But if the Skin be off, there is not any thing in Nature ſo ſure to take out the Fire.

An Excellent Ointment *for a* Pain *in the* Side.

BEAT two ounces of Cummin-ſeed very fine; ſift it, and put to it two ſpoonfuls of Capon-greaſe, and two ſpoonfuls of Linſeed-Oyl; make it hot over the Fire, and anoint the Side with it: Dip a Flanel in the Oinment, and lay it on as hot as you can endure it.

For a Pleuriſy *and* Fever.

AFTER Bleeding once or twice, as there is Occaſion, let the Patient take an ounce of Linſeed-Oyl new drawn; ſweeten it with Syrop of Lemons;

mons; fhake them together 'till they mix, and let this quantity be taken every four Hours: At going to Reft, let them take thirty grains of *Gafcoign-*Powder, with a Compofing Draught. They muft forbear Malt-drink; and take care they do not catch Cold.

This has done great Cures, when taken in time, and will prevent the Diftemper falling upon the Lungs.

For a Loofenefs.

TAKE half an ounce of Hipeca-coanna, decoct it in an equal quantity of Claret and Water; let it boil from a quart to lefs than a pint; ftrain it, and add one fpoonful of Oyl; give it in a Clyfter to the Party afflicted. If the Patient is Weak, or a Child, you muft Infufe lefs of the Root; a Dram being a full quantity for a ftrong Man.

It has Cured the moft violent Ill-nefs of that fort, and was recommended on the Experience of a Worthy and Ingenuous Phyfician.

The

The beſt Way of Burning Claret, *for a* Looſeneſs.

TAKE a large Quart-Bottle that will hold more than a quart of Wine; put to that quantity half an ounce of Cinamon, four large blades of Mace, and a large Nutmeg ſliced; put a Cork into the Bottle, to keep in the Steam, but don't ſtop it cloſe or hard, for fear of breaking: Set this Bottle of Wine and Spice into a Skellet of Cold Water, and let it ſimmer 'till the Wine is a little waſted; ſweeten it with Loaf-Sugar, and drink often, if the Patient have a Cold Decay'd Sto-mach, and no Fever.

For a Looſeneſs.

TAKE an ounce of Cinamon, and as much Ginger; ſlice both ſmall, and ſtrew it on a Chafing-diſh of Coals, over which let the Patient ſit as long as the Fume laſts.

For

For *a* Loosenefs.

TAKE three large Nutmegs, and
the weight of them in Cinamon;
grate and beat the Spice extremely
fine; make it into a moist Paste with
New-lay'd Eggs; dry them in little
Cakes, in a Shovel, over a gentle
Fire: Eat the bignefs of a Half-
Crown, First and Laft, and at Four
in the Afternoon.

Another for a Loosenefs.

TAKE a quart of New Milk, and
fet it on the Fire 'till it boil; then
fcum it, and let it boil, and fcum it
again, as long as any Scum rifes:
When 'tis almoft cold, to the clear
Milk put Two-penny-worth of Aqua-
Vitæ, and let it ftand: 'Twill Jelly,
and keep (in a cool Veffel and Place)
two or three Days. It has done
great Cures.

Cinamon·

Cinamon-Water *for a* Looſe-neſs *and* Fever.

BOIL a pound of Pearl-Barley, and ſix ounces of Plantain-Seed, in ſix quarts of Water; when both are tender, pour it upon eight ounces of Cinamon. Let it Infuſe all Night, and next Day draw it off in a Cold Still: Let the Patients drink of this as often as they pleaſe: If they like it ſweet, put in double-refin'd Sugar.

For a Looſeneſs *and* Gripes.

MIX up twenty grains of Rhubarb, three drops of Oyl of Cinamon, and three drops of Oyl of Juniper, in near a dram of good *Venice*-Treacle; make it into a Bolus, and take it all over Night. Next Morning, in the Working, drink Warm Poſſet-drink in which Mallows have been Infus'd.

This has done great Cures, when the Diſtemper has been very Dangerous.

Another

Another for a Looseness *and* Gripes.

INFUSE a pound of Poppies in half a pint of Spirit of Wine: Take a large spoonful of this Liquor, with six drops of Oyl of Juniper, in a glass of Black-Cherry-Water, sweeten'd with double-refin'd Sugar. 'Twill give Ease in Extreme Pain and Torture.

Note, You must mix your Oyl with the powder'd Sugar before you put it into the Liquor, or 'twill swim on the top, and not mix,

For the same.

PUT a large spoonful of good Plantain-seed into half a pint of Spring-water; boil it half away, and strain it out; sweeten it with double-refin'd Sugar, and drink it All.

It often Cures at once; but must be repeated, if there be Occasion.

To

To Help a Hot *and* Coſtive Habit of Body.

PRESERVE Green Wall-nuts be-fore the Shell is hard, after they have lain a Day and a Night in Water, firſt prick'd full of Holes; boil and ſhift the Water often, 'till they are tender; ſtick in each a bit of Candy'd Orange-peel, and take their weight in a ſweet *Lisbon-*Sugar; boil them up, and take two, three, or four of theſe when going to Reſt.

They are a Gentle, Wholſome, and Certain Purge.

Another.

DISTIL a quantity of Wood-ſorrel-Water in the Spring, and ſweeten it with Syrop of Violets: An ounce of Syrop to a quarter of a pint of Water is a Doſe for any Body, and may be ſafely taken, even in a Fever, or Lying-in: A leſs quantity for a Child.

Another

Another.

ROASTED Apples, with Carra-way-Comfits, eaten conftantly e-very Night, has been the Method of a Gentleman of Fourfcore, who has hardly ever taken other Phyfick, or omitted this for Fifty Years, and never felt the Gout, or Stone, or any other Diftemper incident to Old Age.

Another.

BOIL a few Mallows in one Por-ringer of Water-gruel; ftrain it out, and inftead of Salt, put in a pugil of Cream of Tartar : Let this be your Morning's Draught.

Another.

ONE fpoonful of Syrop of Peach-Bloffoms, taken in a glafs of the Water diftill'd from the Leaves, or in which the Leaves and Worm-Seed has been deco&ed, is a moft Safe and Certain Medicine for the Worms in Children.

INDEX.

INDEX.

An INDEX.

For

An INDEX.

An

An INDEX.

An INDEX.

The

An INDEX.

M.

O.

An INDEX.

Q   *A* Neat's-

An INDEX.

A very

An INDEX.

Q 2   To

An INDEX.

To

An INDEX.

Cherry-

An INDEX.

You may also be interested in these titles:

Townsends is please to make available a growing list of rare and valuable books from the 18th and early 19th centuries, including those listed below. Be sure to visit our website for a complete list of titles.

Cookbooks

The Art of Cookery by Hannah Glasse (1765)

The Domestick Coffee-Man by Humphrey Broadbent (1722) and *The New Art of Brewing Beer* by Thomas Tyron (1690)

The Complete Housewife by Eliza Smith (1730)

The Universal Cook by John Townshend (1773)

The Practice of Cookery by Mrs. Frazer (1791 & 1795)

The London Art of Cookery by John Farley (1787)

The Complete Confectioner by Hannah Glasse (1765)

A New and Easy Method of Cookery by Elizabeth Cleland (1755)

The English Art of Cookery by Richard Briggs (1788)

18th & Early 19th-Century Brewing by multiple authors

The Lady's Assistant by Charlotte Mason (1777)

The Experienced English Housekeeper by Elizabeth Raffald (1769)

The Professed Cook by B. Clermont (1769)

The Cook's and Confectioner's Dictionary by John Nott (1723)

The Modern Art of Cookery Improved by Ann Shackleford (1765)

The Country Housewife's Family Companion by William Ellis (1750)

A Collection of Above Three Hundred Receipts by Mary Kettelby (1714)

England's Newest Way in All Sorts of Cookery by Henry Howard (1726)

—⁘—

Biographies & Journals

The Hessians by multiple authors

Travels Through the Interior Parts of North-America in the Years 1766, 1767, and 1768 by Jonathan Carver (1778)

The Women of the American Revolution, Volumes 1, 2, & 3 by Elizabeth Ellet (1848)

The Backwoods of Canada by Catharine Parr Traill (1836)

Travels into North America by Peter Kalm (1760)

New Travels in the United States of America. Performed in 1788 and *The Commerce of America and Europe* by J.P. Brissot De Warville (1792 & 1795)

The Journal of Nicholas Cresswell, 1774–1777 by Nicholas Cresswell (1924)

An Account of the Life of the Late Reverend Mr. David Brainerd by Jonathan Edwards (1765 & 1824)

Travels for Four Years and a Half in the United States of America During 1798, 1799, 1800, 1801, and 1802 by John Davis (1909)

Travels through North and South Carolina, Georgia, East and West Florida by William Bartram (1792)

A Tour in the United States of America, Volumes 1 & 2 by John F. Smyth Stuart (1784)

—◦◦◦◦✹◦◦◦◦—

Townsends

www.townsends.us